A SHOTGUN Wedding

A SHOTGUN Wedding

The Conflict Between Science and Religion Resolved

PHILIP S. RADCLIFFE

A Shotgun Wedding

Copyright © 2022 by Philip S. Radcliffe. All rights reserved.

No part of this publication may be reproduced, stored in a retrieval system or transmitted in any way by any means, electronic, mechanical, photocopy, recording or otherwise without the prior permission of the author except as provided by USA copyright law.

The opinions expressed by the author are not necessarily those of URLink Print and Media.

1603 Capitol Ave., Suite 310 Cheyenne, Wyoming USA 82001
1-888-980-6523 | admin@urlinkpublishing.com

URLink Print and Media is committed to excellence in the publishing industry.

Book design copyright © 2022 by URLink Print and Media. All rights reserved.

Published in the United States of America

Library of Congress Control Number: 2022919570
ISBN 978-1-68486-311-2 (Paperback)
ISBN 978-1-68486-313-6 (Digital)

18.10.22

CONTENTS

Introduction vii
Book 1:   A Primer on Reformed Christianity 1
Book 2:   A Scientific Baseline 7
Book 3:   The Dialectic Nature of Our Existence 17
Book 4:   The Randomness of Our Existence 30
Book 5:   Illustrations of Free Will in Our Existence 37
Book 6:   God's Creation 45
Book 7:   Who Is My God? 52
Book 8:   God Is the Answer 60
Book 9:   Faith of Our Fathers 66
Book 10: Agnosticism and Atheism 71
Book 11: A Layman's View 80
Book 12: A New View of the Evidence 84
Book 13: Epilogue: There Is a God 87
Bibliography 93

INTRODUCTION

People start companies or write books for one of two reasons, sometimes both: they need money or they have a message. My message is direct. I believe it is more rational and probable that there is a Creator than that we are here as the result of multiple cosmic accidents of infinitely complex precision. The latter is basically the anthropic principle first postulated in 1974 by Brandon Carter, an Australian physicist and professor. This theory is based upon the appreciation of how finely tuned our physical universe is, thereby enabling intelligent life. The conclusion that there is an intellect and purpose behind our unique, or at least rare, existence is constantly debated. Given the new scientific knowledge of the last fifty years, those of us who believe in the Creator must update our theology to incorporate this new and revolutionary understanding of the physical world.

  The title of this book arises from an earlier time and culture in America. A shotgun wedding was a required union in which the groom had a choice: he could elect to make his little darlin' an honest woman or "get his head blowed off." The bride's father was generally the authority who enforced the union. Today, this type of coerced relationship is frowned upon, and I certainly do not endorse taking up arms to make atheistic scientists change their beliefs. However, I do believe that science and religion require a necessary union of mutual advantage and mutual consideration.

Based on things I've read, conversations with friends, and my own continuing quest for meaning in the experience of humanity, I am troubled by the way many scientists and academicians, even those in the humanities, publicly espouse and promote their vision that creation occurred without a Creator. Their concept of existence is of a cosmic accident with no guiding moral value or plan for our existence and future. I never believed that God is merely an alternative to eternal damnation. Like the character Purlie in the musical based on Ossie Davis's work *Purlie Victorious*, I acknowledge that we need some comfort in the here and now. People do experience forms of heaven or hell during their lives on earth, and sometimes that experience is influenced by their personal behavior or mind-set. It is also true that many humans have either positive or negative life experiences that are not solely a consequence of personal choice, behavior, or attitude, which I will discuss in more detail later.

One of my concerns about associating atheism with intellectual activity generally and science in particular is the Judeo-Christian tradition of the importance of the book. Learning gave authority to intellectual pursuits even as man evolved into a being filled with awareness and communication skills instead of one who merely existed at the top of the food chain. The cynical sophistication of intellectual atheism engenders disrespect for the intellectual in many communities and cultures. Most dog lovers have low esteem for a domesticated pet that bites the hand that feeds it. Many people who earn their living in prosaic pursuits may develop low esteem for academics who accept income, even indirectly, from workers paying tuition for their children's education. Conversely, intellectuals dismiss the working community as ignorant. There is a need, perhaps, for someone to act as the father of the bride and wield the shotgun that forces these groups to get together.

Despite continuing market upheaval, I hope that I am able to remain retired with sufficient time to reflect, recall, and record my vision of life. My first book was a memoir about growing up in the Midwest and surviving as an entrepreneur in the high-tech computer industry from 1959 through 2000. My particular expertise was in the field of real-time data acquisition and control, employing computers to monitor and control industrial operations. This background accounts for my respect for science and engineering. I was also my own bean counter, lawyer, and salesman. During my fifty years in business, I have started companies and served as a mentor, early-stage investor, supporter, and director of start-up companies. At least five of the operations still exist either as independent entities or as parts of other organizations. I am still involved with two of the companies and sit on the board of directors of another, an NYSE-traded firm. In my memoir, I spent considerable time exploring my belief in God and continuing my education in science.

In my life, I have encountered Young Earth Creationists who believe that the world is six thousand years old because the Bible, as the literal word of God, lays out generations of begets that add up to that amount. Some of these creationists have college degrees in engineering and have been exposed to mathematics and physics. Some have consulted on major engineering projects around the world. Conversely, I also know scientists of significant international accomplishment who recommend Richard Dawkins or other atheist writers and skeptical materialists as authorities on religious faith. The members of each of these groups usually begin discussions about their positions by discounting alternative points of view.

Young Earth Creationists deny the accuracy of science while skeptical materialists deny the reality of any force beyond physics and chance. I believe these apparently irreconcilable positions must be synthesized in a "shotgun wedding" to ensure our continued presence in the universe. Science and knowledge without consideration of a greater purpose or morality seem to lead to an inevitable increase in the probability of self-destruction as well as our ability to create greater creature comfort on the road to perdition. An attempt to limit knowledge, by limiting exposure to factual expansion that defies some traditional lore, will lead to a weakening of at least military and economic strength and ultimately a loss of credibility. It is also my observation that as our knowledge expands with time and effort, our world becomes more dangerous even as the potential for greater life fulfillment is increased.

The first five chapters of this book are an attempt to "set the table." I begin with a brief review of the reformed tradition of Christianity, emphasizing the reformed tradition because it is the theology with which I am most familiar and because it is an updated view of Christianity, which incorporates most belief predating Luther but modifies those tenets to include more recent adjustments. Next, I discuss the major areas of the expansion of scientific knowledge. From there, I move to the three adjustments that I believe must be incorporated in a new reformed theology.

I focus on how creation seems to have been designed, given the scientific insight of the last fifty years. The universe is a remarkably interactive system that was designed to bring humanity into an environment of inestimable complexity. The reconciliation of science with faith, specifically Christian faith, indeed Christian evangelical faith, has had and will continue to have a fundamental impact on humanity's survival.

BOOK 1

A Primer on Reformed Christianity

I support the school that considers the Bible to be a living text, one that was inspired by God and written, miraculously, by men of limited sophistication, scientific learning, or historical perspective. Nevertheless, they captured divine truth in the scriptures that was relevant not only to their time and culture but also to all times and cultures, including ours today.

The tradition of apostolic succession, which is part of Roman Catholic and Anglican doctrine, limits interpretation of biblical text to those who have been trained and certified as priests. As head of these respective churches, the pope or archbishop speaks with ultimate theological authority regarding the interpretation of the scriptures. Over the millennia, papal authority has significantly affected our definition of the scriptures with consequences for both Protestants and Catholics. For example, under the authority of the pope, Saint Jerome determined which books would be included within the Bible and which books would be regarded as heretical. The translation of the Holy Library known as the Bible has changed from time to time and within different religious denominations. Saint Jerome set the standard for considering content that has become the generally accepted or traditional composition of the Bible and its division into the Old Testament, New Testament, and Inter-Testament books. The

Catholic tradition provides the priesthood with a job description that includes interpreting the scriptures to and for the faithful. This distinction is a root cause for differences today in ritual and practice between Protestants and Catholics, including those related to celibacy, birth control, and confession.

In the sixteenth century, while trying to institute reforms in the Roman Catholic Church, Martin Luther initiated or at least focused on a totally new tradition of scriptural interpretation that ultimately led to a doctrine identified as the priesthood of man. Under this new doctrine, we are each able to generate our own interpretation of the scripture; God speaks to us individually, without the intercession of someone else. Of course, even denominations pursuing the reformed tradition have modified this doctrine to one of corporate interpretation under the guidance of clergy or a synod or general assembly.

These differences in doctrine, ritual, and observation often diminish the credibility of believers, particularly when viewed from outside and have strengthened the position of critics of religion, who attack its relevancy in today's more sophisticated, materialistic, and technologically advanced society. Often the attack arises from the scientific community. In some cases the attack stems from the different systems the scientific and philosophical communities employ when trying to discern truth. Some of the challenges to the credibility of religious belief seem to arise from the supposed advantage science methodology has in distinguishing between proven or repeatable fact and a theory or hypothesis. When scientists discover new phenomena, which in turn may lead to the development of a new or revolutionary hypothesis, they scrupulously avoid making claims about ultimate truth until the phenomena can be repeated within observable laboratory conditions. Thus a current debate in the scientific community about infinitely simultaneous dimensionality under quantum mechanics, while exposing differences among schools of physicists, does not negate the validity of quantum mechanics as a tool in the development of solid-state electronics. It seems that in science we are able to deal with things that we can prove and also deal with and even apply that which we can only hypothesize, without rejecting different hypothesis or different conclusions from similar hypothesis. From a historical perspective, we have to recognize that "scientific truth" in the early twentyfirst century has a very different definition than it did in the late twentieth century. That marks a scant fifty-year time span on a planet that is some 4.7 billion years old.

At times, it seems humanity expects "spiritual truth" to be timeless as well, even as our knowledge about the environment is continuously changing. In *The Case for God*, Karen Armstrong does an admirable job of pointing out how we adapt what we accept to be spiritual truth while humanity's knowledge and sophistication increases with the expansion of written communication. Her observations move from the beginning of recorded history through the growth of monotheism to Christianity.

Perhaps this difference in expectation arises from a single source: the Creator has known us and our environment from the beginning of time. We, however, learn about and come to appreciate Him only over a period of time. Even so, the existence of the God of Abraham is ultimately a binary condition: either there is a single Creator or there is not. If there is one, then quite possibly we can fully appreciate His characteristics and plan only over time as our knowledge of His creation grows. If there is not a single Creator, then our purposeless existence becomes a series of exercises to justify whatever it is we collectively do.

I believe science is a vehicle that demonstrates that our existence was planned and has a purpose, which is the case for any other intelligent life forms within the universe. The primary purpose of science is to help us discover God's purpose for humanity as a whole as well as His purpose for each of us individually. Thus, ironically, if my thesis is correct, the purpose of biologist Richard Dawkins is to lead humanity to a better understanding of our Creator.

In my thesis, I am addressing my fellow Christians who sit in church with me on Sunday morning and make their way in the current world of expanding scientific knowledge. Their daily lives may be affected directly or indirectly by some of this new technology. Most of us only come to appreciate the collective impact of scientific change over time. I want my fellow Christians to appreciate the view that greater knowledge of our physical universe enhances our faith in our Creator. However, new worldviews can require new interpretation of ancient texts, thus expanding our appreciation of the presence of God in our lives.

I accept that there is some degree of chaos and uncertainty in God's design of the universe. The presence of randomness, dialectic conflict, and free will indicate that specific events can occur within a well-thought-out system without specific prior knowledge of the all-knowing God who designed it. I do not find this a conflict. I realize that many will find an acceptance of randomness or other uncontrolled events within God's plan as a heresy that denies His omniscience and omnipotence. I do not accept that a God of all creation, who is aware of each element down to subatomic particles, is primarily an accountant who keeps records on each action and event. I do believe God has established a design, tries to help His creatures follow that design, and even sends emissaries, such as His Son, to redeem us and guide us to reach the potential that exists within all of us.

I recently heard a sermon by my associate pastor, Harold McKeethen, who discussed "sky-opening events." He described how the concept came to him while he was watching July 4th fireworks from the bluffs of the York River, near the birthplace of independence, where General Washington defeated General Cornwallis. At the height of the display, a large cloud from the southeast discharged a huge vertical lightning bolt that diminished the effect of the considerable display of pyrotechnics. It made Harold recall several descriptions of sky-opening events in the Bible: the separation of light and dark in Genesis; the lightning that occurred when God carved the law onto the tablets on top of Mount Sinai; the light of the star that guided the magi to Bethlehem; the lightning during the earthquake and tearing of the temple shroud that divided the sacred from the common areas of the temple; and the description of the events surrounding Jesus's resurrection and ascension. Harold's point was that our current political, economic, and daily conditions are important; God is aware of them and tries to provide guidance and assistance. However, He does not produce sky-opening events casually or frequently. Instead, he works with and through us individually to help us follow His plan and be true to His purpose.

In the chapters that follow I will explain why I believe science has brought us closer to the understanding that creation was planned in anticipation of our arrival. Further, our awareness of history, a subject that we discuss with each other, reveals clues about our purpose within creation. I am troubled that Holy Scripture is sometimes looked upon as both the first rendition of the basis of our Christian faith and the last attempt God made to communicate with His creatures. We still have individual communication with our Creator, and we still have sky-opening events, like when the Hubble telescope recently looked into a dark area of the sky and instead of empty space discovered an estimated fifty billion previously unheard-of galaxies. We are intelligent life forms who are aware of our own existence and have some appreciation for the immensity of creation and the probability that there are other intelligent life forms on what must be billions of billions of planets circling billions of billions of stars. Therefore, we can appreciate that the divine Creator has a job description we cannot comprehend, appreciate, or define. We must be continually aware of new sky-opening events and additional revelations of the Good News.

God has already miraculously provided our earth and our individual existence as gifts of inestimable value, even for those of us who believe we occupy a position of low social consideration or regard. Our task as believers is to use circumstances of grief, pain, and suffering as well as those of affluence, power, and strength to develop the faith to cope with our human existence. If there is redemption and everlasting life in some form, that is a divine bonus, not necessarily a fundamental condition of belief. The Bible states that God made His first covenant with the Hebrews as His chosen people, and the New Testament promises a new covenant with all people and justice in our eternal life. I believe Jesus redeemed all of us with His sacrifice, and He promised a mansion with many rooms as our eternal home. However, I believe one can accept the Creator and a divine purpose without accepting the promise of eternal fairness in an afterlife.

Karen Armstrong is a theologian with an impressive background of social and religious accomplishment. She has posited that science is an endeavor that is limited to defining and controlling our physical world while religion and faith give us the intellectual and emotional resources to deal with nonphysical components, such as pain, grief, and suffering. Her approach is typically theological; she provides a comprehensive analysis of the role of belief from a historical and multicultural perspective, illustrating the role religion and religious belief have played in man's survival as an intelligent and aware creature of God. I believe that the faithful who attend church with me on Sunday morning need to appreciate that religion and science represent different emphases in the effort to understand our world. We have to learn to deal with our total world and continue to discover new truth and reality. Karen Armstrong's books, Francis Collins's *Language of God*, and Paul Davies's *Mind of God* are examples of the modern expansion of the scripture. These books and others represent man's continuing effort to understand our role in the universe given to us by God. Religion and scripture are not static, historic events that happened to our ancestors; they are dynamic realities that keep pace with our expanding awareness of the universe and its potential.

I believe all Christians are called to be evangelists and provide witness to the Good News. I do not use evangelical as a term of practice that eliminates those faithful believers who do not emphasize a born-again experience as part of their declaration of faith. I also hesitate to differentiate between liberal and conservative theology since, in current usage, liberal often includes "new age" interpretation that waters down traditional Christian belief in the redeeming resurrection of the Son of God as the salvation of humanity. The term conservative, on the other hand, is often so constrained that it does not allow for any allegorical reference. The current conservative or fundamentalist school of religion depends on the literal acceptance of each word of biblical text as God's own language, unfettered by human interpretation or translation. If my interpretation of Holy Scripture is correct, it is incumbent on all Christians who witness the Good News to have an understanding of the realities of the world in which God works.

BOOK 2

A Scientific Baseline

I cannot define every scientific understanding existent in our world today. I can, however, itemize some fundamental elements that I believe are generally accepted as factual statements in today's scientific communities. I do this so readers can evaluate our faith in light of the "challenges" presented by contemporary scientific knowledge.

    Let us begin with cosmology and astronomy. The Hubble telescope has enabled us to discover that a red shift can be observed in the spectral signature of light that is emitted from other galaxies. This demonstrates that those galaxies are moving away from us at a specific velocity, which we can use to mathematically extrapolate the instant before the big bang occurred. This calculation is further confirmed by the signature of radio frequencies, observed as static from outer space, that are moving away at a velocity consistent with the creation of our universe some fourteen billion years ago. The addition of some fifty billion galaxies that have only recently been observed might affect the estimated age of the universe, since presumably it would take a longer time or a greater speed to travel the distance needed to make us aware of them. We have found rock samples on the moon where absence of an atmosphere does not alter the composition of meteors that hit the surface from time to time. These rocks are older than any samples on earth. Their dates of origin as well as other measures indicate that our planet is four and a half billion years old. In any event, we have two significant date estimates that seem to reinforce each other in the evidence that the universe and the earth had beginnings and therefore probably will have endings.

We have also observed three general shapes in the galaxies that are visible to us: a discus shape, a capsule shape, and a diffuse, less defined, and almost amorphous shape. Our Milky Way galaxy is shaped, more or less, like a discus. Earth is positioned in one of its swirling arms, which spiral out to form the thin edge of the discus. This places us at a distance from the spherical center with its radiation-emitting black hole. Our sun's distance from the black hole's life-preventing radiation is uncommon in our galaxy but not unique. However, we have not yet observed any planets orbiting other stars in the Milky Way in the more or less circular pattern that is required to provide the relatively stable temperatures that enable life.

Capsule-shaped galaxies appear to have black holes as a primary component. In this circumstance, there seems to be insufficient distance to isolate potential planetary homes required for the development of complex intelligent life. The radiation present at the black hole event horizon and extending to the edges of the shape dominate the entire galaxy.

The diffuse galaxies seem to be dominated by unstable novas and supernovas in which galactic components take shape in a chaotic environment that is unsuitable for the formation of life. Most galaxies that have been observed, maybe as much as 90 percent, are either diffuse or capsular. Thus, statistically, the earth exists in a galactic form that is a small minority of other possibilities. In addition, the earth rotates in an orbiting pattern with other planets in a way that has not been generally observed elsewhere. It is only statistical reality of huge numbers that encourages us to recognize that we probably are not unique. Life has billions upon billions of potential homes, so it is probable that intelligent life forms are somewhere out there. However, it does not appear to be likely that our universe is teeming with intelligent life. As a matter of fact, intelligent life is rare, if not unique, based on all current evidence.

In the biological sciences, including forensic anthropology and microbiology among others, the scope of knowledge has exploded to encompass new evidence and hypotheses that were not previously imagined. Parsing the individual cell to its constituent DNA is probably the most dramatic expansion. We now know that the human has about six billion combinations of the four constituents of DNA in different sequences with combinations that are unique to each individual. Half of the six billion pairs come from each parent, but about sixty pairs are not found in the combination of parental sequences. So an extremely slow and intricate genetic trend does produce different tendencies in a species, but only over an extended period of time.

Darwin's theories of evolution and natural selection predated genetics and DNA analysis. He based his observations on his experiences on the Galapagos Islands and the work he conducted following his expedition. Natural selection is a process in which genes that transmit characteristics that improve chances for survival are favored in succeeding generations, thereby improving the species. The effect of improvement in the survival characteristics of succeeding generations is the basis of evolution. Selective examples have been observed in various species. However, it will require more than centuries of observation to determine how extensive this phenomenon is in determining how species developed and evolved in a broad spectrum. Certain species are genetically more similar to other species and have been lumped into families. Darwin theorized that evolution, employing natural selection, produced a "tree of life" that was subsequently extended to include all species originating from a single cell in the primordial swamps.

Based on both the fossil record and authenticated observation, the earth has experienced billions of species. The vast majority of documented species have existed since the Cambrian period, about 550 million years ago. Thus most of our recorded species originated within a band of time that represents approximately 10 percent of our 4.7-billion-year existence. The slow rate of genetically driven change in our own species and all of the others covered by the fossil record does not, according to Martin Behe at Lehigh University and others, conclusively demonstrate that a slow evolution proceeded from species that existed prior to the Cambrian era. There is no evidence, at least at the present time, to scientifically support a single unique universal developmental process called evolution to the exclusion of other events or causes.

Experiments to create life from chemical elements have excited people from time to time, and periodically someone claims that this science-fiction plot element has occurred. Thus far, no peer-reviewed demonstration of life creation has been substantiated. According to Lee Strobel, a 1953 claim by a man named Stanley Miller, a graduate student at the University of Chicago, has specifically been refuted.

Two examples of "scientific truths" employed by most materialists cannot be repeated, fulfilling Popper's criteria for fallibilism in which one negative observation destroys an unscientific theory. First, there is no conclusive evidence that life emerged from the introduction of an electrical charge into a chemical slurry. Second, evolution has been observed within a species, but neither evolution nor natural selection explains the introduction of any species let alone the existence of all species in the mythological "tree of life." In addition, there is the reality of irreducible complexity where it can be demonstrated that many different cells do not have a primitive antecedent from which they modified into their current state.

Karl Popper (1902–1994) called himself a critical rationalist. He used fallibilism to differentiate true science from social science. Under this concept, a single instance of fallibility or contraindication would prove a scientific truth invalid. Popper had problems with theoretical physics and in particular with the theory that solid bodies could cause light to bend. He might have seen Einstein as just another scientist who solved a problem theoretically and then gathered data to provide a good narrative. Except he recognized that: one, if no future observation proved relativity invalid, its effect would be revolutionary; two, many scientists would spend their careers looking for the single example of fault in the theory. I can only imagine what Popper's reaction to quantum mechanics would be.

Popper attacked social science theories on the basis that they cannot be proven valid or invalid. He believed that because a theory in the social sciences can be modified to accept invalid examples, it is amorphous or of little worth. Science, in contrast, looks for a single case to prove a theory invalid. Popper indicated that social science proponents represented man's age-old desire to prophesy. What Nassim Nicholas Taleb in *The Black Swan* calls the narrative fallacy is in Popper's experience the bias, particularly among social scientists, to gather only data that validate a well-told theory, ignoring the more significant cases that disprove it.

The point of this review of evolution and natural selection is not to refute these theories but rather to demonstrate that neither one meets the rigorous test of proven science. Theories can be employed within science just as statistics can be used to define probable cause. However, again referring to Popper, until a theory can be reduced to a repeatable laboratory discipline, it remains a theory even when it is the best explanation given the limits of our knowledge at this time.

I recently viewed an excellent PBS program in 2012, a part of its Nova series I believe, that was dedicated to the effects of stress. The program focused on four specific areas in which studies have produced significant conclusions. The first area was the medical evolution of the cause and treatment of peptic ulcers. The second area was the work of a college professor who studied various baboon tribes or congresses over an extended period of time. The third area included a review of the published results covering 24,000 British civil servants. The final point was a study of a large group of mothers, both married and single women, who were caring for their profoundly handicapped offspring. I found the observations particularly interesting and significant.

In the first case, the program discussed society's move from the belief that ulcers were caused by stress to the discovery that the sores were bacterial infections that responded to antibiotics; ergo, ulcers were infections. Eventually, medical science determined that bacteria are present in most people all of the time. The apparent cause of the infection is a breakdown in the autoimmune system that is caused by . . . stress. It seems to me that this progression represents a circular path of observation, with "truth" revealed in different ways at different times.

The baboon study was more complex and extensive covering the majority of the presentation time. Baboons are complex social creatures, typically found in hierarchically arranged troops or congresses that are headed by an alpha male or small group of alpha males. The scientist took blood samples and blood pressure measurements over many years within several different groupings. He found that incidences of high blood pressure, obesity, or diabetes, all diseases linked to stress, decreased the higher the subject stood in the hierarchy. Thus the alpha male at the top of the tribe had lower indications of stress than a submissive young female of breeding age at the bottom of the hierarchy. One tribe, which was studied for more than twenty years, discovered a food source of human garbage that contained tubercular infested food residue. The alpha males and their immediate subordinates dominated the food distribution and consequently fell victim to tuberculosis. After some time the tribe suffered from a short-term loss of breeding alpha males. The surviving males, rather than excluding themselves from the responsibility of parenting their young, developed a revised social order of a more egalitarian model. The new order has been maintained and the observed incidence of diabetes, high blood pressure, and obesity has been reduced overall, indicating a reduction in stress associated with the new and apparently unique social model observed in this singular congress.

Then the program discussed interviews with 24,000 British civil servants, the results of which seemed to parallel the baboon experience. The higher one stood in the civil service hierarchy, the fewer symptoms of stress one exhibited, as indicated by time off due to illness, high blood pressure, and diabetes. The interviews reinforced the conclusion that high-level civil servants felt little job-related stress while well-educated but lower-level civil servants were frustrated with their jobs and experienced more frequent time off due to reported illness.

The final report was on female caregivers attending their profoundly handicapped offspring. This study seemed less complete and, as I recall, did not report on an extended set of observations. The primary finding was that coping ability was enhanced when the women attended support groups, after which they experienced a reduction in the feeling of aloneness.

My reasons for discussing the PBS program are multiple. First, the "scientific" study of both physical and psychological health, employing statistical techniques, physical measurement and close observation, can develop different true interpretations depending on expanding knowledge in related fields over time. Second, since this book is concerned with interpreting our Creator's purpose for our design and existence, these experiments and observations reveal some apparent realities about our existence: We deal better within ourselves when we are hammers and not nails. We deal better within our societies when we are in supportive groups. Our physical being is improved when stress is reduced even when the environment remains physically unchanged or at least not materially revised. However, I wondered why none of the examples dealt with the question of the effect of religious belief. I can understand that this issue might not be significant in the baboon example, but I wonder at possible effects in the other cases involving humans directly.

Moving from evolution and sociology to more recent developments in the biological sciences, we are in the infancy of stem-cell research. Some day we might trigger a generalized stem cell to develop into a specific cell such as that in a liver, brain, or heart. Stem-cell technologies as well as the continuing expansion of our knowledge of DNA and genetics promise both the extension and improvement in the quality of life. However, we must take care not to extrapolate either a known phenomena or a logical but unknown extension of current knowledge into a future truth that may or may not occur. Enthusiastic extrapolation can quickly become faith in a future reality that may or may not come to pass. Enthusiastic extrapolation of evolution transformed natural selection almost into a religion and into realms that Darwin himself probably would not accept.

We have reviewed cosmology, astronomy, biology, and genetics. We are now ready to look into physics and discuss current "truths" that have modified our worldview. While much activity and progress has occurred in physics during the last fifty years, the research into subatomic particles and quantum mechanics has projected science into the world where mass and energy become fuzzy. Today, the Large Hadron Collider (LHC)—a physically massive device, some nine miles in diameter, built for the purpose of colliding protons, among the smallest particles of mass we can currently measure—is still in the early phases of start up. It was scheduled to operate through 2011 prior to a shutdown and upgrade in 2012. A primary mission of the collider is to isolate, measure, and track Higgs boson, a theoretical massive particle that has not been previously detected and a fundamental element predicted by Einstein's Standard Model, which defines all of creation. The laboratory presence of this particle would substantiate much of the mathematics supporting the Standard Model. (Higgs boson is a highly transient byproduct of colliding particles. Its presence represents support for the explanation of producing mass from energy. It has been referred to as the "God particle" in the media primarily because it defines how a collision of two particles can produce other particles and energy that transforms into mass for at least a fraction of time.)

Particle physics is the driving force behind solid-state processor development. The ability to contain memory elements and logically operate on these elements via increasingly complex algorithms requires ever diminishing geography on each element or chip. This space compression reduces the distance signals travel between elements. The physics predicting the behavior of subatomic components of the chip enables continuing miniaturization. Moore's Law, a theory proposed by the CEO of Intel in the late 1960s, stated that the number of transistors on a chip would double every year. By 1970, the time constant was increased to every two years. We are at the threshold where within the next decade or two, a transistor will be down to around ten atoms or less. At this time we cannot foresee going much beyond that primary limit while employing silicon as the ingredient of single chip processors. This limit will focus our attention on alternate processor material such as carbon nanotubes or else the progression could end with computer processors only one thousand times more powerful and physically smaller than today's most advanced microprocessors. Development of more capable processors with essentially infinite memory and increasingly responsive networks represents breakthrough technology in the development of more "human" robots complete with language skills and emotions.

Today, special purpose computers interpret measurements and modify the operation of our vehicles and provide ever more elegant entertainment centers. In February 2011 *Time* magazine had a cover story discussing the evolution of computers and robotics to the "point of singularity" when there will be no distinction between human and machine. The article suggested that 2045 would be the date when this would be observed, based on such recent events like the debut of IBM's Watson, a computer that can interpret voice and nuanced text questions in the popular TV game show *Jeopardy* and respond with answers more proficiently than the best available human competitors.

For many years, physicists have been seeking the algorithm that can explain everything. The Standard Model, as developed by Einstein, has twenty-three constants of unexplained origin and gaps at the subatomic level where particles bond. The existence of these gaps is more readily explained by some variant of string theory. String theory and its extensions and variants work pragmatically to predict subatomic behavior; however, it requires acceptance of unobservable multiple dimensions resulting in the improvable hypothesis of multiple universes each unaware and unaffected by each other's presence. A theory that statistically predicts results that conform to a probability adjusted pattern does not meet requirements of the scientific method for repeatability and consistency. That is not to exclude its practical value in providing a protocol to follow in application.

The behavior of miniscule subatomic particles where mass and energy seem to merge is a limiting factor on how powerful computers can become. This domain of the subatomic realm is also the key to enable the modification of the action of DNA in individual cells to either fight or prevent disease. Subminiaturization (nanotechnology) is our stepping-stone into the world of more healthy, intelligent, and long-lived humans who will most likely be composed of a hybrid combination of biological, mechanical, and electronic components.

Today's frontier of artificial intelligence (AI) and heuristic modeling of the human brain, combined with the growth of processor power and the unlocking of the triggering mechanisms of DNA, offers a very different possibility for life just one hundred years from now. Working in this frontier, it is easy to become seduced into a belief that we can control and either establish or impede any and all characteristics or conditions of humanity. The atheists among scientists end up rejecting the idea of God and instead support the extension of the miraculous developments we have thus far discovered to project a new materialistic and technological brand of faith.

In the fall of 2011 the scientific community announced the observation of a previously impossible condition: neutrinos were observed to move faster than the speed of light. If this were a reality, the Standard Model, Einstein's answer to all creation, would lose its validity. I do not appreciate the implication that at least some subatomic particles move faster than the speed of light. I recall that Einstein's theory contained as a postulate that movement at speeds faster than the speed of light involved regression in time. The point of this excursion is to illustrate that even highly accepted scientific theory can be superseded by new discoveries of what always existed but was beyond our ability to observe and measure. The calculations supporting the speed of the neutrinos recently have been shown to be flawed. However, since Newton's theories still are applicable except beyond a certain scale, perhaps Einstein's theories will become limited by our ability to view the complete physical world at some time in the future.

BOOK 3

The Dialectic Nature of Our Existence

Some fifty years ago I took a college philosophy seminar on dialectics, the unity of opposites, that discussed the German philosopher Karl Friedrich Wilhelm Hegel (1813–1901). The seminar explored how Marx and Engels used dialectics to develop their concept of class warfare. My acceptance of the dialectical nature of reality in most aspects of our existence is based upon Hegel's formula of thesis, antithesis, and synthesis as well as my reading and observations. I am not concerned here about employing the dialectic technique to examine all metaphysical principles. Rather, I will focus on the observed reality that all existence occurs within a joining together or synthesis of opposing forces. These contradictions seem to be a common characteristic in observable creation.

In the following sections, I will examine dialectical behaviors in the physical world, organizational and political tendencies, attitudes toward economics, and perceptions of the supernatural and religion. My point is to demonstrate my definition of the dialectic nature of our existence. I am sure that I will fall victim to Taleb's narrative fallacy since my effort will be directed toward validation rather than fallibilism. At the age of seventy-five I am interested in validating my own observations, and I will leave the continuing search for fallibility to those who want to look for a more universal scientific truth than what we can currently experience.

Dialectic Influence in Our Physical World

Everyone needs to spend an evening far away from the polluting effect of city lights. Armed with a pair of quality binoculars, look up into the sky and admire the heavens. You will find it to be a very humbling experience. The pinpricks of light that are visible overhead belie the statement that more than 90 percent of the universe consists of dark matter. It seems instead that the heavens are filled with nothing but light sources. It is impossible to feel that what you are looking at is history. But some of the light you see as you gaze heavenward began its journey to your eyes millions of years ago. Undoubtedly, some of those pinpricks of light no longer exist as light emitting bodies by the time you can view them.

We exist in our families and homes, neighborhoods and communities, and nations and the earth in a universe so vast we cannot comprehend its dimensions. Light travels at 186,000 miles per second. In a year, light travels 186,000 miles × 60 seconds × 60 minutes × 24 hours × 365.25 days. Much of the light we see travels for millions of years until we see it for an instant, and a second later, that light is 186,000 miles beyond earth.

Sound travels by exciting molecules in our atmosphere and compressing and decompressing against surfaces that are sensitive to the frequency changes. At six hundred miles an hour, it moves slowly enough for us to see images on our TV screens before we hear audio unless it is synchronized via amplification and relaying. We diminish the delay by converting sound to digital signals that are transmitted at the speed of light and then converting them back to sound near its destination. In open spaces, we can see a flash of lightning well before we hear a report of thunder because light moves so much faster than sound.

At one time, the field of quantum mechanics was driven by the quest to understand how light travels. Einstein theorized, and it was subsequently demonstrated, that light moving by a solid body bends under the effect of gravity. Therefore, most scientists presumed that light moved like sound from particle to particle, but with particles reduced to the subatomic level so light transmission could move swiftly. We are still exploring the world of subatomic particles, specifically now driven in their application in computers. We are also researching forces such as light, gravity, electro-mechanics, and other secrets of the universe. The LHC illustrates our continuing quest for additional knowledge.

This expansion of our knowledge—through vehicles like the LHC and the Hubble telescope—confirm that our physical world was built and is maintained by the existence of opposing forces. The night sky demonstrates an order maintained by the centrifugal force of the earth's spinning orbit that pushes us away from the sun even as the sun's gravity pulls us closer. The resulting stability is caused by these forces opposing each other. In biology, we learned that some measure of our existence evolved as a result of competitive influences that employ natural selection. Evolution is demonstrated within species, human and others. I rely on these examples for my support of the dialectic: examples of actions moving in opposition to each other, resolving into a condition of imperfect unity that may be revisited from time to time with different outcomes.

In *The View from the Center of the Universe*, Joel Primack and Nancy Abrams point out that the various models of physics—from Newton's to Einstein's to quantum mechanics—are not necessarily different paradigms; rather, they are extensions of earlier paradigms. Thus Newton's observations of the earth were "stretched" to Einstein's view of the universe, which was devolved to our current nanotech level of subatomic particles. To my eyes, this is an observation of scale serving as the synthesis that resolves apparent contradiction of a different thesis to a unity, bounded by the scale in which you are working. Our current exploration of space is dominated by Newtonian physics, not cosmology or quantum mechanics.

The gap in a continuous evolution from single-celled creatures in the primeval slime to billions of living species that currently exist is complicated by the archeological evidence. Based on that evidence, we know that at least twice in the roughly 4.5 billion years of the earth's existence, most species were wiped out and evolution started down a modified route, a phenomenon that illustrates a step-function change outside of the hypothesis of slow, steady progress. This evidence of step-function changes in our progression to intelligent life supports the premise by Lehigh University biology professor Martin Behe that genetic mutation cannot account for all of the species on earth, living and extinct. DNA modification and natural selection also do not explain the irreducible complexity evident in selected single-cell examples that could not have evolved from a previous "simpler" creature.

On the other hand, 4.5 billion years is a long period of evolutionary development, and much of it is confirmed by the fossil record. The work of Francis Collins at the National Institutes of Health and others has shown that DNA can establish evidence of both parental and sibling relationships.

However, children have approximately sixty unique genetic mutations that cannot be traced to either mother or father. The sixty unique combinations do not arise from the combination of two genomes of about three billion base pairs each, one genome each from one's biological mother and father. There is evidence of evolution, such as the DNA database illustrating the distribution of humanity from our first Homo sapiens ancestors in Africa, across Asia, Europe, and even over the land bridge to the New World before the continents drifted apart. However, this evidence does not infallibly support a science of evolution. Indeed there are still debates about genetic admixture between early Homo sapiens and European Neanderthals or simply a species replacement. The lack of specific evidence for how all individual creatures originated, the triggering factors in the rate of genetic change over time, and the scale we are dealing with provide major holes in all-inclusive evolution through natural selection.

While difference is not equal to opposition, and therefore may not demonstrate true dialectic characteristics, it certainly does illustrate a difference even within the direct link of genetic relationships. There are several other illustrations that indicate how opposing phenomena produce the results necessary to sustain life.

A SHOTGUN WEDDING

Our turbulent atmosphere produces destructive storms. Yet we require that stormy atmosphere and the resultant circulation of air to support life on a large scale. The same life-sustaining storms sometime terminate life in individual cases. Our increasing awareness of the value of tropical rainforests and our dependence upon polar ice caps illustrate the limits of our habitable earth. We need carbon dioxide to be converted to oxygen through photosynthesis in plants so that we can breathe. Our environment, from atmosphere to resources, is complex, and we need to research how to better practice good stewardship. However, we should not hypothesize about cause and effect; rather, we should establish known and repeatable evidence before we upset either the established natural or economic balance with potential major consequences.

Contradiction and even competition are fundamental elements of our physical existence. I recognize that it may be a stretch, but I equate competition with a controlled resolution of contradictory forces that meet in a managed environment. In a cosmological example, heavy atoms arise from the conflagration of dying stars that give birth to self-aware life forms. As *The View from the Center of the Universe* points out:

> Each of us is an atomic pastiche: the iron atoms in our blood carrying oxygen to our cells came largely from exploding white dwarf stars, while the oxygen itself came mainly from exploding supernovas that ended the lives of massive stars, and most of the carbon in the carbon dioxide we exhale on every breath came from planetary nebulas, the death clouds of middle size stars a little bigger than the sun. We are made of material created and ejected into the Galaxy by the violence of earlier stars, including some supernovas that exploded before the solar system formed four and a half billion years ago and some that happened only a few million years ago. To understand how that happened—to appreciate the millions or billions of years it takes a star to

> produce a comparatively tiny number of heavy atoms, and the tremendous space journeys of those particles of stardust that have now come together to incarnate us—is a first step toward feeling some conscious contact with what we are made of and our cosmic history.

The life of our planet and indeed our lives upon it are born of the death throes of other heavenly bodies. Indeed we are composed, at least in part, of stardust as well as DNA.

Of course, the mammalian reproduction system is to some extent the ultimate example of the unity of opposites. Female concavity complimented by male convexity is an example of perhaps opposites but definitely differences. In his book *The Selfish Gene*, Richard Dawkins cites the difference between a single egg produced cyclically over days and targeted for attack by millions of sperm produced in hours as a possible genetic predisposition for the female as nurturer and the male as philanderer, since females have more invested in their eggs than males have invested in sperm. Of equal significance, mammalian gestation and its climax in birth is a female experience. So the very survival of our species, as well as almost all mammals, is a result of synthesizing differences into a common singular outcome.

Dialectic Influence in Organizations and Politics

The influence of the unity of opposites is printed on our money, e pluribus unum—"out of many, one." The United States has a system of checks and balances that we export to many nations of the world. Our democratic political system is built on the concept of the loyal opposition. Our judicial system is built on the principal of advocacy in which two sides to any dispute present their case and receive judgment from peers or from the bench. This process is a controlled environment that allows both civil and criminal litigants to synthesize their differences by accepting the outcome recommended by the legal system, though a price may be paid by one or both parties.

Our games are built on friendly competition under a set of rules, and we maintain records of wins and losses to determine league or world champions. Many games are series of meetings in which each outcome has significance, with cumulative wins and losses serving as measures of the relative result, at least for the season. The act of victory is a form of synthesis. It may not resolve all issues for all time, but it does produce a decision that is sufficient for the time being.

While those in the arts do not compete with each other directly, only a select few artists do secure the brass ring of success, whether it is by selling paintings, records, or books. Talent alone does not always determine who is or is not successful. Timing, promotion, and sponsorship can differentiate between the wealthy and influential and those who merely earn a living. Success is not the only criteria for "winning," but it does resolve who in the short-term gains the most influence.

Our corporate structures are responses to regulations, competing organizations, and internal differences from which we hope that superior goods and services will be provided at best possible advantage to the consumer. The role of sales and marketing is typically the task of translating customer needs in terms of an organization's products and services and providing feedback to improve the products and their position in the market. Hopefully, finance and accounting keep product design and distribution convenience under economic control to ensure the survival of the enterprise. This corporate cooperation is yet another example of a mutually desirable result driven by competing influences in a civil arrangement. These examples in organizations, politics, and business are practical exercises in analyzing the effect of competing differences in controlled circumstances with the victors in each case enjoying a transient synthesis of success. Sage and experienced participants in any of these arenas recognize that sometimes the synthesis of success can be a pleasant but far from total or permanent resolution.

PHILIP S. RADCLIFFE

Dialectic Influence in Economics

Initially I was going to include the following observations in the previous section. But given our current economic distress, I decided this topic was worthy of its own consideration. Once again I find it beneficial to review my interpretation of Hegel's definition of dialectics. Dialectics is the process of identifying opposing forces that can synthesize into either stability or a period of resolution. Hegelian dialectics require mediation. Free-market economics are built on the principle that the market is the ultimate mediator. However, no one in today's environment, which was developed over centuries of experience, understands a free market as a totally laissez-faire and unregulated institution, though there is sharp disagreement about what degree and severity of regulation are necessary. It is distressing to hear heated debate with little tolerance for other points of view when people are discussing the role of government or individuals in our economic well-being. Often prosperity for the vast majority of citizens of nations or the world is the desired outcome of both parties; yet the debate frequently is more than animated.

I find it disappointing that an eminent theologian like C. S. Lewis considered socialism to be his favored Christian answer. He based his very European observation on the fact that capitalism advocated competition, which he found to be mean. Competition in a civil environment is not mean. It does produce winners and losers, hopefully in an effort to winnow out the preferred solution at the time. Most often multiple solutions succeed simultaneously with some organizations more favored than others. It is our human empathy for the loser that seems to make it desirable to accept a mediocre or egalitarian outcome rather than a long-term superior outcome that would develop as a consequence of good efforts that may not survive the test of market acceptance. We feel bad about individuals who put forth effort that is unrewarded or less rewarded. It is difficult to appreciate in the near term that the better result in the longer term would positively benefit a far greater part of society, including consumers and likely labor, management, and owners as well.

History demonstrates that in a pure laissez-faire system, civil competition is often the exception rather than the rule. We have witnessed the use of performance-enhancing drugs in the field of sports entertainment. It is difficult to know how many teammates actively or passively participated in individual violations of good sportsmanship let alone league rules. Yet not all NFL linemen consumed steroids. Many rejected the drugs out of a sense of self-respect and self-preservation that concluded anything powerful enough to be effective has to have deleterious side effects.

Most of us know from childhood that there is no such thing as a free lunch. You ultimately pay a price for decisions that introduce stress to your psyche or body. I know of no individual who was a starter in college football for several seasons and who does not bear, by age fifty-five or so, some evidence of the wear and tear on his body. The price may not have been fully appreciated during youthful participation because the passion of the moment and economic incentives were compelling. However, the player knew his body was taking a beating, and somewhere in the recesses of his mind, he knew some price might be extracted in the future.

Our best experiences in economics seem to underwrite a combination of freemarket competition with a minimum of regulation, with the market mediating the preferred solution(s). There will always be crooks who profit by defying the system and who get away with it for some time. Most heavyweight participants in our economic activity are intelligent, hard working, honest people who were ready to take advantage of lucky breaks that they saw, while their contemporaries did not see them or pursue them successfully. Many of the "losers" in our entrepreneur-loving system also benefit from their less than successful attempts. Indeed, studies have indicated that many successful people failed during their first attempts. Most people in the United States are not extremely affluent owners, managers, or independent entrepreneurs. Most of us just do our jobs as best we can, even if we have some mutual fund shares in our retirement accounts. In a civil environment, competition has enabled more of us to realize a superior level of economic reward than was ever before witnessed in history. Trickle-down economics, imitating noblesse oblige, is not a desirable solution. Yet the burdensome taxation on the construction of luxury yachts, purchased only by the wealthy in this country some years ago, drove thousands of New England artisans and craftsmen out of business and out of work.

Free-market proponents seem to have a historically compelling case for providing a supportive and minimally regulated environment to encourage the development of competing and voluminous operations, some of which fail and some of which succeed. Planned economies with the presence of governmentally designated operations "too big to fail" have a history of limited success in terms of providing products and services delivered to and produced by their own citizens. The product of a less efficient collection of independent smaller operations seems somehow more efficient at a practical level than a directed and unified effort from a centralized political operation. Even extensive businesses cycle through periods of organizational centralization and decentralization, motivated by efforts to increase coordination and decrease waste and redundancy while improving responsiveness to local demands or rapid changes in requirements.

The preceding observations are additional examples of opposing influences in our economic environment. Over a reasonable time period, a collection of decentralized, sometimes redundant operations can be more efficient than a single, integrated organization. More people end up employed by a collection of smaller organizations than are employed by the largest organizations in the nongovernmental workplace. The decentralized private sector provides the revenue base that ultimately generates all goods and services, including those nominally supplied by the government.

Dialectic Influence in Religion and the Supernatural

If our physical world, organizational structures, and economic systems are built on opposing forces that in effect provide stability, what about our spiritual and religious experiences? This discussion can be approached on several different levels, including the forces opposing religion or belief and the opposing forces within religion—the age-old issue over who is the true believer. I do not consider science to be a force that opposes religion, though there are many scientists who personally oppose religion as a form of supernatural rationalization. I also do not believe that Satan is God's evil twin and antithesis. I agree with Rev. Rob Bell who, in his book *Love Wins*, proclaims that he cannot accept that a loving God would condemn anyone to an eternity in hell, a kingdom ruled by Satan. In scripture, the first commandment states that you should not worship any other gods beside "me." If we create, in the same scripture, some other supernatural creature with godlike powers to oppose God, have we not committed the Gnostic heresy of creating another god? I believe this is but one example of human influence in the Holy Scripture. The Holy Bible contains truth but as presented by the human authors who wrote it. These writers are subject to errors of interpretation in both the original presentation and further in the translations over the centuries. Assuming there is no evil supernatural being, what are the forces opposing belief?

I will not present a television version of the top ten reasons a universal religion is not accepted. By contrast, I have found it interesting to hear from several sources that the skeptical community that denies religion—i.e., atheistic scientists—spends more time reflecting on God and His involvement in the world than many believers do. So I would have to begin my own short list with the God-given defense mechanism of skepticism. This is a natural tendency to view any positive offer with a sense of disbelief, particularly an offer of redemption that can improve one's attitude toward life. Another hill that belief has to climb is the human limitation of scale. We cannot comprehend either the massiveness or the minutia of the elements in our environment, let alone all of the interactive relationships that are present during each microsecond of our existence. There is also our collective tendency to find it difficult to acknowledge our own worthiness for accepting both the corporate and individual loving concern of a supernatural Creator. Any problems introduced by our difficulties with skepticism, scale, and worthiness are opposed by unconditional acceptance and love. Evil does exist, but it is most often the dark side of a positive attribute: skepticism that denies the reality of sacrifice and altruism; ambition that sells out to greed and self-centeredness; loving concern that is twisted into control and subjugation; freedom without the restraint of responsibility. The positive side of our individual and collective character is fragile and almost without our awareness, it can go "round the bend" and obsessively become sinful behavior.

One solution offered by religion is discipline. While some call to order seems necessary if we are to follow an interpretation of God's spiritual will, most often this discipline becomes a rite that separates "us" from "them" without the recognition of the fundamental commandments to love God and each other. In his best-selling work *God Is Not Great*, Christopher Hitchens describes several different religious dogmas and points out the ritual differences among them. He then employs these differences and conflicts to attack the validity of faith in any supernatural existence. The obvious differences in believer's rites are used by several atheists to characterize all religion as narrow, exclusive, and unforgiving.

The founder of the world's largest religion, Jesus Christ, is probably the strongest example of a spiritual leader who opposed the organized religions of his time—Judaism and polytheistic Roman worship. While faith has many values in common, there are seemingly irreconcilable differences in the tenets of religious belief and in denominational rituals and rites. C. S. Lewis observed that religion in general and Christianity in his experience seem to spring from that universal experience of humankind to know what is right and a desire to behave in an acceptable fashion such as dictated by some form of the "Golden Rule." Lewis also pointed out that there is a human tendency to feel guilty about doing things that are contrary to our better nature. All religions teach regard for others and some form of love as desired behaviors, and yet there have been more people slaughtered as a consequence of following their religious leaders than any other collective cause of conflict in the history of humanity.

The Judeo-Christian tradition is book driven and seems historically to give support and encouragement to scientific research and expansion of knowledge, despite periods of clerical suppression or denial of worldly knowledge. Islamic tradition does not seem to produce the same irrepressible desire for knowledge about God's creation, at least not as it has been practiced since the sixteenth century. Modern Islam, particularly its more fundamental traditions, relies on the belief that all activity of this world is a consequence of Allah's will. This approach of faith ruling knowledge is more in common with fundamentalist Christian and Orthodox Jewish traditions. I find a religion that denies our God-given desire to learn as much as we can about the universe in which we exist is a denial of God and an attempt to put boundaries on His intellect.

So there is an observable tension of opposing forces both toward the acceptance of any faith and within the practice of various branches of faith.

BOOK 4

The Randomness of Our Existence

We have just reviewed how contradiction and the unity of opposites are basic elements of our physical, organizational, economic, and religious institutions and stabilizing forces that maintain order and organized interdependency. I believe God introduced chaos and randomness into this order. Nassim Nicholas Taleb has written several books dealing with randomness in life, using examples from the financial market to illustrate his point. His primary point is that random, not statistically predictable, events have major impacts on our lives and the market. Chaos is one reaction to random events that amplifies their occurrences. Chaos also occurs as individual events in nature —the unpredictable effect of debris flung about the universe as a result of the ongoing birth and death of heavenly bodies, such as stars or galaxies. It seems to me that chaos is also a fundamental component of this creation in which we live. If our universe was created by God, He created the dialectic and randomness as well. Unlike Einstein, I think that God does roll the dice, at least from time to time.

If it is not true that some events occur randomly but every event occurs only as a result of God's will, then that suggests that God is capable of generating unimaginable events of cruelty or His omnipotence is limited in the presence of opposing gods like Satan.

Consider the possibility that randomness is a designated palliative that was built into God's system to make inevitable bad events in a temporal and competitive environment more acceptable and even viewable as potential opportunities during which people can learn about and express God's love and control at their highest level. Pain is a designated biological warning system of impending danger. If pain is a consequence of our bodily and emotional systems requiring feedback to avoid selfdestruction, then C. S. Lewis's book *The Problem of Pain* is a more believable explanation of positive attributes in a negative experience. This observation is mine since Lewis does not propose that pain is a random event but rather that it is a learning experience with profound positive outcomes, either now or in the hereafter.

My point is that as fundamental components of God's design, chaos and randomness are consistent with a system of competing forces, a dialectic presence, and free will—our self-determined selection of a course of action. Imagine a Creator confident enough of His design to empower creation itself and its self-aware, intelligent beings on the earth to have measurable impact on the outcomes of at least pieces of His creation.

Randomness in Nature

In *The Black Hole Wars*, physicist and author Leonard Susskind points out that when two Planck-length strings—theoretically the smallest unit of mass —pass through each other, there can be several outcomes: They can continue through each other with no apparent effect. At the point of intersection, the top halves of the two strings can become a new string while the bottom halves similarly become a new string. Finally, the new strings can be either closed or open. Those are five different random outcomes for the single phenomenon of two subatomic particles intersecting in space. The outcome can be statistically forecast if sufficient quantities of these intersection events are present and they can then be employed as practical applications in our current silicon-dominated, semiconductor world. Many classical physicists do not accept that mathematically predictable outcomes can be a substitute for a true explanation of this apparently random phenomenon, which might someday be readily repeated and measured in a laboratory. As nanotechnology becomes a necessary domain for continued semiconductor advances, this statistical approach probably will not be sufficient. Yet Stephen Hawking, this era's preeminent physicist, did finally use a form of string theory to accept the theoretical and mathematical evidence that explain how bits of information, i.e., bits of energy and mass, were not lost in a black hole.

Thus at the smallest level of mass in all of creation, the simple act of intersection has a truly random outcome. At the other end of the scale, an asteroid measuring approximately ten stories high recently missed the earth by some forty-one thousand miles. There is archeological evidence that such a collision occurred more than 500 million years ago and ended the era of the dinosaur. We are aware of the random paths of many asteroids and the conflagration of space dust flung out by stars in their death throes. In our midsized scale, we find that children have DNA codes related to the combination from their parents, but they also have sequences not traceable to either parent. These observations seem to indicate that several examples of unpredictable things can happen in nature without the clear prediction of either an individual event or the combined outcome of several events. What we have seen over time is that unpredictable or random events are part of our existence.

Randomness in Our Organizations and Institutions

Our recent history includes companies like W. T. Grant, Westinghouse Electric, Montgomery Ward, and Lehman Brothers, none of which are still around. The causes for their demise and the timing of their difficulties were different, and some of those companies still have remnants in operation. The private sector is littered with the skeletons of many large enterprises that were at one time considered stable organizations. I have often heard that as many as nine out of ten smaller commercial operations fail within one year after startup for a variety of reasons. At the time of their demise, most of these organizations had three- to five-year forecasts illustrating how their activities would grow in volume and profitability. Some failure was due to ineptitude, improper financial control, or low-quality products. Some failures seem to occur in spite of adequate capitalization, good management, and solid performance; sometimes, failure just happens. Most organizations are not described as "too big to fail." Their success or failure is generally regarded as the risk of business. Success seems to need good fortune as well as good management.

The observation that success is often, if not always, a product of luck as well as preparation and skill reflects Taleb's emphasis on randomness. Twenty years ago, I made a judgment based upon my comfort with a company's principals and their approach to a particular field of technology and decided that their efforts merited investment assistance. After passing through a couple of merger and acquisition activities, it appears that this investment will yield almost a 3,000 percent return before taxes when some escrow funds are released this year (i.e., 2012). This was not my only investment in earlystage technological ventures, and not all of those investments turned out this successfully. This success does reflect some discriminating capacity on my part to select an early stage operation with a higher probability for success. However, I am confident that the principals—whose return on invested equity was greater than mine but whose return on effort was significantly lower than mine—would also agree that good luck and favorable turns of fortune had a heavy impact on the outcome.

Randomness in Our Economics

Nassim Nicholas Taleb was once a successful trader on Wall Street. His book *The Black Swan* discusses the impact of the highly improbable. Among other points, he attacks current portfolio risk-analysis techniques that are built on observed statistical performance of past behavior, and discard events outside of usual patterns. He points out that both upside potential and downside risk are more affected by occurrences of the infrequent and highly improbable than the projections of any forecasters. Of course, events since the financial crisis of September 2008 seem to substantiate at least his downside riskmanagement analysis.

Bill Gates is brilliant, and by all or at least most accounts he is a deserving entrepreneur who now enjoys the fruits of building Microsoft, one of today's dominant technology ventures. In 1980, he sold IBM on using his small, new operation to complete the development of a Disk Operating System (DOS) for its emerging new personal computer, a bulky desktop device with limited capacity that sold for around $10,000, equivalent to $50,000 to $100,000 today, given the inflation of the last thirty-plus years. Converging developments in technology—computers, communication, and increasing appreciation of the value of information—drove costs down and demand up. This does not suggest that Gates and his associates were only lucky and otherwise without intellectual skill and commercial abilities. However, without what was an unpredictable course of events in the 1970s, all of the intellectual and commercial skills possessed by Gates and his associates could not have led to Microsoft becoming the dominant operating system software supplier since the mid-1980s. Gates certainly demonstrated effective management abilities that enabled Microsoft to take advantage of its good fortune, and that is a skill set common to most successes.

Random good fortune is not the only element necessary for a successful enterprise. However, without good fortune, it is extremely rare, if not impossible, to build a successful enterprise. Many successful businessmen have attributed foresight to their ability to succeed, and some have an arguable case. Many if not most, have enjoyed blessings that could not be predicted. Certainly, Thomas Edison was one example of an entrepreneur who seemed destined to succeed, based on his intellect and breadth of interests. He likely would have affected history, no matter in what period he lived. Statistically, I believe there are fewer examples of commercial success that reflect Edison's prescience rather than reasonably competent people being in the right place at the right time.

Randomness in Religion and the Supernatural

On one hand, this is a difficult subject for illustrating areas of randomness, since religion is built on an internal reliance on steadfastness. On the other hand, challengers of religious belief often point to the seemingly random nature of God's hand in worldly affairs. This concept is usually discussed shortly after they point to the absence of an omnipotent being during extensive periods of human suffering, whether those affected are individuals or groups (e.g., epidemics, the Holocaust, and other genocide). The nonbeliever certainly presents a strong argument by focusing on circumstances where humans would intervene but God apparently does not. The toughest question is, *When Bad Things Happen to Good People*, also the title of a book by Rabbi Harold S. Kushner.

Traditional Christian theology looks to the resurrection that was promised as the ultimate solution to fairness and justice for innocent victims of bad things. Surely if the Creator and His Son went through scourging and the Crucifixion to illustrate His promise of redemption, such ultimate salvation must be available for each of His individual followers. There is historical evidence for this doctrine, including the words of contemporary witnesses who suffered for their testimony and evangelism. This faith in redemption cannot be scientifically and empirically proven since it would require observable repetition and for transcendent experience to be physically evident. However, the doctrine of redemption also cannot be disproved. One indication of the strength of belief, according to the faithful, includes the many people who have chosen to die to maintain the validity of their faith rather than to live by rejecting it.

Randomness in God's creation is similar to having the devil loose in the candy store. How can an all-knowing and all-powerful Creator compromise His being by enabling any portion of His creation to go off on its own in a less than completely controlled fashion? Yet doesn't the existence of the free will that God gave to man ensure that unpredictable outcomes will occur? In my experience, I have seen evidence of unpredictable and improbable events occurring repeatedly and often with cruel effect. I am left with the conclusion that either God is trying us, or things occur as a systemic component that still allows God to empathize with us, love us, and support us even in the throes of our misfortune. I cannot conceive of an all-powerful Creator intentionally killing, for example, a mother and child during a complicated childbirth, and still claim to love us. I can more understand the Creator dealing with death as a necessary component of physical creation and enabling a systemic physical death as inevitable for each member. In this sense, randomness is a palliative, making dying, in any fashion, at any time, more acceptable to us.

BOOK 5

Illustrations of Free Will in Our Existence

As I've read some of the works by Carl Sagan and Richard Dawkins, among others, it has become evident to me that gifted scientists are actively seeking scientific laws that can be applied consistently within our natural environment. Moreover, they have developed a scientific methodology that consists of a hierarchical arrangement of hypotheses and theories as well as truth and facts. For example, string theory is still not accepted as mathematically true, but perhaps once we receive the results from the new LHC, we will be able to demonstrate the theory's validity in another way.

Based on the works mentioned above and others as well, it appears to me that scientists interpret the theology of predestination in this way: an all-knowing and all-powerful God is aware of what will happen before it happens. The logic seems consistent with a hypothesis that a being with the knowledge of the Creator will know everything that can or will happen. This connection is very different than a hypothesis that proposes that the Creator has given the elements of his design independent capability that might modify or terminate His creation.

The ability of an individual to select a course of action from among several alternatives, particularly when one does not have complete awareness of the long-term consequences, is certainly one definition of free will. The same ability to choose even when one is aware of the detrimental effects is an even more dramatic illustration of the same free will. While predestination suggests that the choice and its consequences are already known to the Creator, physical evidence suggests that surprise is often a reaction to choice. Thus physical observation, the keystone of proof in science, is rejected by the scientist who requires predestination of a Creator.

I am not aware of the personal circumstances of Sagan and Dawkins during the periods they wrote books in which they addressed the existence of God.

Sagan's *Varieties of Scientific Experience* is a compilation of the Gifford Lectures he gave in 1985 when he was around fifty-one years old. Dawkins wrote *The God Delusion* in 2006 when he was sixty-five. *The Selfish Gene* was first published when he was thirty-five. In my brief look into Dawkins's biography, I discovered that he apparently had a daughter with his second wife with whom he lived for eight years until around 1992. My point is to note that at least at the time he was writing, neither scientist had apparently experienced a relationship with a mature adult child, i.e., one over the age of thirty, the type of relationship most frequently referenced to explain Jesus's connection to God and God's relationship with humanity. It is possible that their reliance on the concept of predestination and its implied total control might have been tempered if they had been parents of adult children, a relationship in which parents have influence but lack complete control. This does not suggest that only parents of adults can appreciate or understand God's relationship with us, but it does point to a level of appreciation that grows with the experience.

At the age of seventy-five, I have reached the point where my adult children are dealing with the complications of maintaining relationships with my grandchildren, who are now approaching adulthood. The point of this discussion is to provide firsthand experience of an example of free will within the parent-child environment. A parent who seems omniscient and omnipotent to his infant or young child realizes that his offspring needs to exercise some degree of free will as she progresses from puberty through college, until she is almost entirely independent. As our children mature to independent, self-supporting adults, our lives are enriched by a relationship exercised within the bounds of free will and mutual respect. Choosing to love each other in a friendship that approaches total equality—economically, intellectually, and socially—is the most fulfilling experience of our lives, and has provided me with insight on a human-value scale that Sagan and Dawkins did not have while they were writing their books.

This discussion will present my observations of the existence of free will within our physical, institutional, economic, and religious worlds.

Free Will in Nature

Illustrations of free will in the universe have to be limited to examples of intelligent beings, and even so the issue of free will versus genetic predisposition can be debated. I believe that altruism is a primary example of free will, in which an intelligent being intentionally acts unselfishly and contrary to his own apparent best interests. Other choices might include a life's work, athletic participation, or a spouse. Whether choices represent the exercise of free will, are genetically preordained, or the result of social pressure from peers or family can usually be determined after the fact. However, even retrospection may not fully establish motivation. In legal cases, we decide motive based upon observed action. For example, the distinction between first-degree murder and manslaughter can be indicated by the purchase of an insurance policy with the accused as beneficiary, particularly if it was recent and there are limited reasons to indicate this was a usual and customary occurrence. During certain periods in my life, I chose to play football and participate in requisite exercise and required training while at other periods I decided not to play and undertook other activities. Later in life, football was no longer a choice for me because the physical demands of the sport could no longer be handled by my body.

As married adult children with children of our own, my wife and I elected to pursue career opportunities in communities some distance removed from our parents. We valued our relationship with parents and siblings and chose to make sometimes inconvenient and high-cost visits to see them. Our families likewise chose to visit us multiple times per year and continued to do so as long as they were healthy enough to travel. Even if the sense of family and the commitment to maintain physical contact is a genetic predisposition, at a minimum there is free will exercised with respect to timing and logistics. Funds availability, condition of vehicles, school or social calendars, and other events generally present in a busy yuppie lifestyle will affect the range of choices in each situation. But it is free will that moves us to maintain those family ties despite the potential inconvenience.

My wife and I chose to adopt and gladly pursued it as a source of some of our children. We made our choice without knowing that we would have biological children in the future. We find no distinction in our feelings, reactions, and inclusiveness toward our children and grandchildren. No doubt there was some pressure on us as a young married couple to produce a family, but it was extremely subtle at most, particularly compared to the pressure we put on ourselves. We truly desired, out of a selfish need to provide for others, the opportunity to be parents. Fortunately, we had the experience both of adopted and biological children, who are now adults.

Free Will in Organizations

The illustrations of free will in community, business, religious, and social organizations become the choice of whether or not to become members of those organizations. In our neighborhood within a broader community, there are currently fifty-plus organizations, ranging from bid whist, bridge, and wine and dine clubs to those focusing on travel, computers, and theater. In addition, we enjoy opportunities in the extended local community to engage in volunteer efforts and take higher education courses and seminars on various topics. By contrast, membership in the armed forces, law enforcement, and other first-response organizations, while initially voluntary, become fixed commitments owing to the nature of the tasks these organizations fulfill. Business affiliations are generally a mixed bag of membership by choice and of necessary advantage in carrying out a designated duty. Some examples in the business domain might be professional and trade associations.

In each example, there is some question about how free is free will? In *The Selfish Gene*, Dawkins seems to suggest that attitudes and inclinations are primarily predetermined by genetic characteristics. For example, he goes to great length to promote the idea that altruism is a genetic predisposition to preserve the species. His ultimate stretch is to cite game theory as a support for self-sacrifice. While there are examples of cultural bias toward either selfinterest or selflessness, there are also examples in which individuals choose not to follow the prevailing pattern. The individual's decision to accept prevailing wisdom or choose an independent course represents, in my opinion, free will. Business-related decisions are at least to some degree determined by the compensation advantages ascribed to each choice. Certainly free will does not have to be present without any other unelected influences to still represent choice, but where the line gets drawn becomes a matter of personal value and belief.

Free Will in Economics

As in various organizational institutions, free will in economics ultimately comes down to the decision "to buy or not to buy." Salesmanship is intended to encourage the buyer and make it easy to say yes. Even socialist states have ever-present black-market and bartering activities that exist side by side with the centrally controlled marketplace. Communism tried to control supply and therefore consumption. Demand seems to have more staying power and eventually will give rise to an unauthorized market presence. While boycotts have been employed from time to time to pressure suppliers, they generally only work for a short time and usually break down.

The United States has tried to employ the boycott as a tool of foreign policy from time to time but, in my opinion, with limited success.

A peculiar benefit of the effect of collective free will as exercised in a free market seems to be a driving force to improve the choices that are available to all. Economies with a controlling central authority and where wealth distribution is a political decision seem to breed corruption and lost opportunity. In the free-market case, the breadth of choice may seem inefficient, wasteful, and rewarding only to a select few. However, when production capital, such as union and teacher pension funds, is owned by many, the rewards flow back to vast numbers in our society.

Ultimately, free will is not evident in every action we pursue. Advertising, word-of-mouth references, economic incentives, and occasionally direct orders certainly influence decisions we make daily. Moral and cultural values are also direct influences. According to C. S. Lewis, a voice of conscience is present in every human even though daily we read about heinous acts committed by someone seemingly without conscience. Is that an indication of free will or of missing genes? Perhaps some of each. Acts of the deranged are just that—oddities evident in small samples of humanity and either genetic deficiencies or bad acts with no excuse or rational explanation. Free will, however, is evident in many if not most acts in which people engage. Free will is not involved in breathing, pulse rate, or perspiration; though one's mental state can affect all three biological actions. In economics, the issue is, can the market introduce the same effect as the biological compulsion to breathe or have one's heart beat? While we do need to consume food in some minimal quantity, most consumption occurs as a choice rather than a requirement. Choice can be influenced, but ultimately it is a personal decision for which we individually must accept responsibility, even in a regulated segment of the market.

Free Will in Religion

Recent efforts to discover, define, and understand the brain, challenge the traditional view of humanity as a dual being—part physical and part spiritual. MRI, CAT, and PET scans indicate that in most people certain stimuli, whether visual, auditory, or written, evoke predictable activity in certain regions of the brain. This activity, combined with increased understanding of the neural network's electro-chemical activity, has enabled scientists to postulate that pure mental activity is the source of all of our imagination, creativity, and reasoning. This extension of observed fact into a more generalized conclusion is similar to the school of thought that foresees DNA manipulation as the way to eliminate all human imperfections and frailties. There is no question that our expanded knowledge of brain activities and body chemistry will yield improved treatment of our frailties and deficiencies. This reality does not preclude the possibility that humanity includes an undefined spiritual origin.

Historically, science has developed solutions to problems but has fallen short of achieving a total response in the manner predicted. It seems that each discovery unfolds more unanswered mysteries. Einstein's Standard Model of creation does not hold together if neutrino particles move faster than the speed of light. The same is true when Newtonian physics are applied beyond the realm of our planetary system. There may be limits to our ability to discover the ultimate truth. Within the limits of what we currently know, it seems that the soul can still exist within our physical being. It is the extension of our current knowledge that hypothesizes the demise of the soul. I don't believe that will ever come to pass because our Creator designed a soul as a basic component of our existence.

The ability to discriminate between cacophony and harmony, the appreciation of the western sky at sunset, and the bonding of a newborn with its parents are moments that transcend physical awareness while still including the physical stimulus. Yes, it is possible to rationalize that all mental activity, including emotion, is electrochemical. It is not possible at this time to create a predictable thought or reaction within a developed or a developing mind. We have discovered that the brain is not an arrangement of miraculously fast individual components but rather an amazing combination of parallel processes that accept and interpret sensory data while simultaneously determining if the data are of no threat or are desirable. Where does thinking begin and sensory input diminish?

I believe that most of us accept that our reactions to certain stimuli can be predicted. I believe the lines separating predictable reaction from differentiation between stimuli and very rapid inductive or deductive reasoning can vary by individual, and I accept that some of these distinctions exist more in the eye of the beholder than as measurable events. Within this complex pattern of independent mental processes and predetermined reaction, we individually make choices about how we respond to our world. That world includes the individual decision to believe or not believe in a Creator or a Supreme Being. Some of us believe that within the complex issue of redemption (which can include the potential for eternal damnation) there is another component, the fear of God, which is a limit on our free will. I accept that Christ died for all our sins, and if we accept Him in faith and the acts we do, we will be given redemption as a birthright. This enhances the value of our choices in the eyes of our Redeemer because we were not required to accept Him as a condition of our lives now or in the hereafter. So in my belief system, free will enhances the value of our faith and actions, even when we know that the best of us cannot earn our own redemption.

I believe that contradiction, randomness, and free will are integral components of an evolving creation initiated, managed, and redeemed by a Creator who possesses intellectual and emotional capacity that is beyond our ability to comprehend. We can appreciate His gifts, but comprehension of them is beyond our pay grade.

BOOK 6

God's Creation

This creation we live in is at once so vast and so miniscule that it is incomprehensible. Yet science strives to seek the truth about why it all works. Each discovery, like the peel of an onion skin, uncovers yet another puzzle. Einstein's theories of mass, speed, and time are limited by the speed of light, yet scientists recently thought they observed subatomic neutrinos covering a measured distance at speeds greater than 186,000 miles per second. Subsequently, this measurement was called into question. If it should stand, there will be another reevaluation of what currently appears to be scientifically valid. The recent discovery of a five-thousand-year-old human body in the Alps revealed via DNA analysis that this person had Lyme disease and ate a substantial amount of food consisting of both grain and meat. Scientists were at least somewhat surprised to see how little genetic difference there was between this specimen and a modern-day Spaniard, the nationality he resembled most, despite a span of 250 generations. While five thousand years is only 0.001 percent of the period that goes back to the Cambrian explosion, given the observed rate of change in 250 generations, is that time period sufficient to explain all the billions of species observed since creation?

We know that miniscule differences in the atomic structure of elements found on earth would make our self-aware human existence impossible. Despite the recent progress in technology, including improvement in direct measurement and detection, we still lack fundamental knowledge of the workings and interactions of either massive bodies or tiny components. Yet they all work together in a choreographed dance that includes us and all living and nonliving components of this vast universe. If we assume this was all put in place for our benefit, does that necessarily mean that only pleasant experiences are beneficial and only positive events are to be allowed? It would seem that a fixed creation consisting of a set population might be structured in our imagination to be an ideal place where nothing bad happens and resources match demand so that none are in want. Once that idyllic concept was corrupted by death and competition, problems of duration, distribution, and fairness crept into Utopia. Yet are we not by our very nature invested in using our efforts, time, and talents to manage our world? Didn't God allow us to choose whether or not to participate and ensure that our errors would threaten only a corner of His total creation? Isn't the Creator so invested in His creation that He designed vehicles to participate in its continuous development? We tire of continuous challenges yet are bored by extended moments of satisfaction. If we have all we need but our neighbors, those terrible Joneses, have one smidgeon more, we may be motivated by envy to move beyond our needs to our desires. This point was made by Karl Marx in one of his pamphlets, *Wage Labor and Capital*, which seems to totally destroy his thesis, "from each according to his ability and to each according to his need."

What did our Creator create, or as important, what did He not create? Did He create evil, sin, or Satan? Why do innocents suffer? Why do good people experience evil? Why do evil people sometimes fare quite well according to the material standards of our earth? Is there a Satan, God's evil twin? I look to the first commandment of the Judeo-Christian covenant that there are no gods other than our God. The Creator would not, in my belief, create His own antithesis. So what is evil? We know it exists, and we have experienced some degree of it at one time or another. I believe, to paraphrase Walt Kelly, creator of the comic strip *Pogo*, we have met Satan, and he is us. Our individual or corporate desire for power, physical comfort, and unrestrained physical sensation can motivate us—individually or in gangs, tribes, communities, states, and nations—to act immorally and pursue our short-term pleasures regardless of the cost to other humans who are not part of our group. Once our own tendencies, which in different circumstances might ensure our survival, become perverted, they can become motivation to bring pain and suffering to others. If we are not in the group creating pain and discomfort, we have often been among the apathetic that do not come to the aid of the afflicted.

To be sure, the forces of nature do from time to time hurt people, and as the population continues to grow, more people are hurt as a consequence of population density regardless of geography. Maybe climates are more severe, or maybe it is just that more of us are exposed each time a natural disaster occurs. In any event, bad things sometimes happen that are not caused by people and seem to be without malice and only part of the usual and customary violence of nature. In these "acts of God," the same phenomena of turbulent storms that produce fresh water we require for existence can and do produce climatic violence, death, and destruction. The 2010 earthquake in Haiti was a consequence of tectonic dynamics associated with the earth's molten core, a fundamental element of our gravitational stability maintaining order in our planetary system. Other accidents occur as unintended consequences when a sophisticated society produces or moves goods and services over systems we humans develop. These accidents can be caused by individual acts of carelessness or negligence, or they may occur as random failures of materials or restraining and controlling systems. Misfortune is not the same as evil, but if you are a victim it is sometimes difficult to distinguish between them.

So we have motivated evil or human-caused harm, forces of nature, or random accidents that can cause grief and pain. Isn't there a better alternative? C. S. Lewis wrote eloquently about his experiences of growth and learning through his personal exposure to grief and pain. He did not conclude that God sent pain and grief to teach us lessons, but that it is our challenge to employ these unavoidable experiences—born of the conflict of free will, randomness, and the presence of opposing forces—to become better Christians, remembering the suffering we imposed on the Son of God and how He employed that travesty to redeem all of humanity. We cannot appreciate His sacrifice unless we learn through our own experiences how He kept his commitment and conquered material limitations to save mankind. Very few of us are called upon to face anything like crucifixion and scourging with full awareness of what is coming.

We have free will to practice good stewardship of our earth and act as God's partners or continue uncontrolled breeding, begging for our own destruction in significant numbers from storms, epidemics, or incidents created by humanity. The dilemma of God, consistent with His design of our creation, is similar to the limit we mortals face with our own adult progeny. The issue in my opinion is how we view control. We do not control our adult children but we often influence them. We try to use the childhood and young-adult phases of their lives to help them make grownup choices. If God developed beings that ultimately had to do His bidding, the value of His relationship with them would be no different than our relationship with an infant or a pet. However, while I believe God has ultimate control, I also believe that He is a guiding force who encourages us to treat His creation, including each other, with responsibility, concern, respect, and consideration. Sometimes we find our potential, and behave in a manner consistent with His guidance.

I recently finished reading *Bonhoeffer: Pastor, Martyr, Prophet, Spy* by Eric Metaxas. Dietrich Bonhoeffer was a Lutheran theologian born in Germany in 1907. Though he was offered a position at Union Theological Seminary in New York in 1937, he returned to Germany and actively conspired in attempts to assassinate Hitler. Bonhoeffer was executed in 1945, just a few months before Germany's surrender.

Bonhoeffer spent his final eighteen months in a Nazi prison. From his earlier published material as well as his writings and communications with survivors of that period of imprisonment, we have insight into many of his theological concepts, including his view of the relationship between God and humanity. Certainly as a pastor, Bonhoeffer believed assassination was anathema to a loving and redemptive God. Yet he accepted treasonous assignments from the Abwehr, the German military intelligence service, which hid his conspiratorial efforts from the Gestapo. His biographer explains this contradiction by defining Bonhoeffer's view of Christian life "as something active, not reactive. It had nothing to do with avoiding sin or with merely talking or teaching or believing theological notions . . . It had everything to do with living one's whole life in obedience to God's call through action." Life "was not a cramped, compromised, circumspect life, but a life lived in a kind of wild, joyful, full-throated freedom—that was what it was to obey God." Hitler was the personification of evil, and it was God's will to see him stopped in his tracks as soon as possible.

The positive strength of Dietrich Bonhoeffer's faith and intelligence enabled him to continue his efforts to confuse and misdirect Nazi efforts to get to others through him and to maintain a positive approach to his constrained existence. The circumstances of his life seem to be an example of both free will and the dialectic nature of existence—a prisoner choosing to live a "wild, joyful, full throated freedom" by being obedient to God. Can a Supreme Being who knows what should happen give individuals the gift of accepting or rejecting His or Her desired path to fulfillment? Are we God's interactive partners in His creation, on which we can have negative impact regardless of His planned outcome for our civilization?

This life of examined faith also seems to superficially beg the question of the ends justifying the means. Did Dietrich Bonhoeffer justify unchristian action through blind faith? What differentiates him from the jihadist terrorist? First, Bonhoeffer examined his faith daily and discussed with others the problem of being a Christian, and a pastor no less, but participating in plots to kill an evil dictator in contradiction to God's command to love our enemies. He worked for change during the early 1930s prior to Hitler's full dictatorial grab of power. It was only after his awareness of the slaughter of Jews and the Nazi invasion of and slaughter in Poland that Bonhoeffer concluded, with great difficulty and much soul searching, that Hitler's acts made him evil incarnate and a justified target for elimination. In addition, the plots to eliminate Hitler did take care to minimize the chance of harm to bystanders. Today's jihadist purposely seeks to ensure the slaughter of a maximum number of innocents— so-called infidels—

to gain maximum attention. I believe the degree to which one examines one's actions within the tenets of one's faith as well as the care one takes with relatively uninvolved innocents can differentiate justification from fanaticism.

The issue of the ends justifying the means is an area of legitimate examination of every act of humanity. However, I am taken aback by people, including several atheistic scientists, who employ the argument of imperfect design to demonstrate that all is random chance. According to this criticism, God, if He existed, surely would have done a better job of designing the universe. I believe this arrogance represents trivial argumentation not examination. I was particularly disappointed to hear Bart Ehrman describe himself as an agnostic on NPR on June 18, 2009, after spending thirty years in scholarly study of the Bible. He came to the conclusion that each biblical author wrote about his own experience and to his own culture. This diversity of authorship convinced him that the Bible was not dictated by God and was not the inspired word of God. The tipping point in his decision to label himself an agnostic, while criticizing atheists as people who are unable to prove their position, seems to me to be based on his evaluation of God as a divine engineer who should have developed a better system.

If we begin with a blank sheet of paper and set out to design a universe, we begin with a first question: do we want a static universe with a set population matched to its environment, having no worries about basic needs or health, and possessing eternal material life? Or do we want a universe of transient occupants who have free will and a temporal existence and make independent determinations about their circumstances, including governing systems, and are devoted to increasing their knowledge about their own existence and the "secrets" of their universe? If the size of the population varies, space must be made available through some vehicle such as death. If people must die to make room for others, there must be some redeeming pleasant experience that motivates people to get on with their lives. Love seems to be the primary positive ingredient.

A static condition versus a dynamic condition is a binary choice. Our dynamic reality requires constant change, an uncertain condition. Unless there is some positive experience among our transient states, we will elect to either reduce or stop reproduction rather than forcing subsequent generations to face nothing but fear, torture, and ugliness. Beauty is a positive feature. Comfort is another. Aging is a characteristic that makes death more acceptable.

Without making an all-inclusive list of positive and negative characteristics, we can conclude that such a list could exist. Furthermore, our definition of good or bad can be contextualized and expanded to consider death as an alternative to ongoing suffering, or blindness as a vehicle that inspires individuals to maximize other talents, such as music. Without exercising much imagination, we can see that good and bad become something other than black or white. Indeed the same activity could appear on both lists, depending upon context and circumstance. The basic determination is whether the universe and specifically our earth were created as dynamic and changing or as a steady, static environment populated by a single population with no addition or subtraction of members.

Given that our experience is of a dynamic environment, we can now consider the specifics of humanity's trials in this creation

BOOK 7

Who Is My God?

"My God" is not used here as a possessive term but rather to introduce others to the God I believe in and pray to daily. I can know and have a personal relationship with the God I believe in, yet I cannot comprehend the scope of His domain or intellect. I believe the Bible—which has, for example, a story of creation in Genesis that is almost totally parallel to a Babylonian myth— contains truth that speaks to modern man even though I do not believe it was literally written by God, word for word. I do believe writers and translators of the Bible thought they were telling God's story, and in parts the Bible retells what its authors believed to be history. However, the Bible's primary purpose is to pass on everlasting values from prophets, apostles, and disciples and ultimately to lead us individually to claim the redemption God's Son gave to us.

    The Bible is an educational textbook. I have little doubt that stories in the Bible could vary significantly from the accounts of an eyewitness. World War II histories reflect the different memories of various eyewitnesses. That does not mean WWII didn't happen, I know it did; I saw POW trains with German soldiers pass our house. However, I'm sure my recollections of the war, even with my readings since then, would be very different than those of my childhood next-door neighbor, who barely escaped with his life and had a German bullet imbedded permanently in his heart during the Battle of the Bulge in December 1944. The Bible is one of God's vehicles for imparting how we should live in harmony with His creation. Our variance from His lessons almost inevitably costs us at least discomfort. Even in harmony with His teaching, we still have to deal with systemic realities, including our own demise and that of those dear to us.

Skepticism seems to be a fundamental human characteristic. It is a defense mechanism that protects us from schemes, scams, and cons that could otherwise cause us harm. Among the twelve selected disciples, one was a betrayer and one was an outspoken skeptic. I believe that lurking in each of us there is a bit of Thomas, whose doubt we would like to allay by examining the wounds and verifying that something familiar stands before us. This lingering doubt has been expressed in at least two contemporary novels whose plots involve secret evidence that Jesus was not resurrected with resulting consequences on the established church and its assets. Similarly, a PBS special discussed the discovery of an ossuary in a Jerusalem graveyard containing bones of a Joseph, Mary, Jesus, and Mary, Jesus's wife. These bones are not complete skeletons and their identity cannot be specifically traced to Jesus of Nazareth. The TV program is yet another example of a hypothesis arising from a doubting population. The evangelical Christian community often emphasizes the absolute necessity that the tomb was empty, as the resurrection story describes. I cannot argue with the ultimate necessity of this event as the proof that God is with us. As I previously stated, I do not hold that Jesus's only value was the resurrection. His teachings involve a pattern of living with God's creation as well as the promise of redemption in an everlasting afterlife.

At some point, skepticism, if it remains despite all evidence to the contrary, becomes denial, which is a negative and often harmful reaction. I find the testimony of several eyewitnesses recorded in the New Testament as well as people's ongoing belief for more than two thousand years—based upon a collective experience even in the face of torture and death—compelling evidence of the presence of the Son of God among us. If, in the face of this reality, individuals continue to deny His existence, I believe they are limiting their opportunities to have a rewarding existence in this world and participate in God's redemption as announced and demonstrated by Jesus.

So, let us meet my God. He reigns over the entire universe and all the creatures on its billions of planets. He is not confined to the earth though we are. He exists simultaneously across millions of light years, and is aware of and involved with all creation, but particularly those planets where life in any form exists and, most particularly, where intelligent life can be aware of His creation. Recognize also that I employ He, Him, and His as a matter of convenience not to indicate the gender of our Creator.

In a memoir I wrote, I went to lengths to estimate that six billion individuals might equate to a layer of pencil points of about 0.216 inches in diameter, or about 21.43 dots per square inch, spread one point deep across the floor of a ten-thousand-square-yard sports stadium. God can know and communicate with each point simultaneously. I also recognize that statistically there are probably at least a billion planets in our galaxy that might have an atmosphere that supports carbon-based life forms. We now project that there are billions of galaxies in our universe, and there may be multiple universes. The God of all creation is conscious of each component of His creation and is still capable of having an individual relationship with each of His created forms of life at whatever level of evolution they are.

I can describe characteristics that I believe are attributable to my God. I cannot comprehend how He can be that vast and possess a level of discrimination that enables Him to communicate with each of us individually. But He can understand me even if I cannot fully appreciate Him.

I can appreciate that an individual engaged in scientific activity either academically or in a private endeavor can be reluctant to acknowledge a God, since it might seem an easy answer to the deep questions about how our world works. The Islamic example of "the will of Allah" as a replacement for intellectual curiosity has been given elsewhere as an explanation for the few Muslims among Nobel laureates in physics, chemistry, and mathematics. In my opinion, a true believer in a Supreme Being must address the question of whether God exists and what are His nature and intent. I do not believe that the only acceptable proof of God must come from repeatable laboratory experiments. Further, I cannot comprehend my Creator standing still for that level of skepticism, multiplied by billions of individuals on billions of lifesupporting planets. I do not consider a scientist to be enlightened if he rejects out of hand the existence of God because He does not choose to respond to the tests of a statistically insignificant sample among the beings He created. Furthermore, as Darrel R. Falk points out in *Coming to Peace with Science*:

> Richard Dawkins extrapolates from the data of science to conclude that life is a blind product of DNA molecules—purposeless, with nothing behind the scene except vast empty space. How does he know this? Has he done experiments to test this? Extrapolation may work within the natural world of test tubes, graphs and computer modeling, but how can it be used to move from a world governed by natural laws to make conclusions about a world of Spirit—a world that supersedes the natural? Dawkins uses extrapolation to jump out of the realm of science and into the domain of philosophy—hardly a scientific way to use a scientific tool.

Let us consider that 14.5 million years ago the big bang seeded an everexpanding universe with components that were transformed into what we are today. The bang not only required great amounts of mass and energy but also the process that changed the explosion into an organized universe. Indeed, there are likely multiple universes, all of which started with their own bangs and probably not simultaneously. Given our understanding of atomic structure and physiology, there is a logically defendable position that intelligent life in the cosmos most probably consists of beings of about our scale that are similar electrochemically to us. The issue is whether this is all a matter of random chance or whether our existence was planned.

In my technical industrial experience, systems, processes, and complex assemblies of material cannot be created without prior planning, a significant design effort, and frequent missteps, which are measured against objectives and corrected before solutions can be achieved. Consider for example, the US and the international space exploration program. We still cannot define exactly where our efforts might lead in the long term, but we are proceeding in what we perceive to be a well-thought-out, planned program, adjusting our progress to fit our experience as we gain it. While I do not accept the concept of a six-day process occurring six thousand years ago as a historically accurate representation of how creation occurred, I also cannot appreciate that creation was a random accident with no design, purpose, or dynamic component. I find that the model of parenting can be an analogue of our relationship to God. We generally define our relationship to God as like that of a parent and her children. We achieve our greatest satisfaction when our offspring exhibit intelligence, good judgment, patience, and skill in their achievements. Is it not reasonable that God, our Father, in whose image we exist, would experience similar satisfaction in our positive achievements as well as sorrow about our foolishness? We do not predetermine our children's future. We try to prepare them and demonstrate the value of a positive program, but they execute their own lives in a continually evolving and modified environment.

The parent-child relationship, while it varies among species, is a common model for living creatures. I noted earlier that Sagan and Dawkins had not had this experience by the time of their writings that I read. If those learned gentlemen had adult children, they would not have used bad behavior done in God's name—e.g., atrocities driven by religious fervor—to determine whether God exists. We do not sentence a murderer's parents to prison, because our experience has demonstrated that we are each responsible for our own behavior. Parents have influence but not control and certainly not absolute control. I can thereby accept that my God will not always exercise absolute control but will hope that He can exert positive influence and education upon his offspring.

A SHOTGUN WEDDING

What about miracles? Did God encourage His Son to perform miracles that defied the laws of physics and chemistry? The God who created our cosmos is fully capable of sending His Son as an emissary to humanity on the earth and elsewhere. The Son of an omniscient, omnipotent and omnipresent God who maintains a personal relationship with all intelligent life in His cosmos would not dictate our performance and behavior any more than His Father does. Similarly, the Son would not be constrained by our "laws of nature" any more than His Father was. Yet the Father is not capricious, and will not defy His own system arbitrarily, or why would He have bothered to establish a system and order? At any point, He can stand above His creation to serve a higher purpose or communicate with his progeny. "Beloved, are we not the children of God?"

We are still left with the overarching question of why God's system of life is full of inconsistencies that we cannot reconcile with the behavior of a loving parent. Why are babies born in Darfur when they will be condemned to death from disease or starvation? Why is there a disease that genetically afflicts only Jewish people in such a debilitating and currently irreversible fashion as does Tay-Sachs? Where is His justice? Why are many apparently good people afflicted with sickness or deformity?

I do not need the experience of food poisoning to empathize with a victim of that malady. A choice of a place to dine generally includes consideration for apparent cleanliness and knowledge of the reputation of selected establishments. Reasonable people generally consider the consequences prior to making choices. I can appreciate that if only good things happened to good people, our free will would be compromised to the point of nonexistence. While it has been observed that the offspring of negligent or abusive parents can and often do still love their parents, the probabilities seem to favor children of loving parents returning the love they experience. This is not to suggest that God is sometimes abusive, but rather that He employs randomness as a vehicle to make the temporal nature of His creation bearable. People are sometimes abusive as a consequence of their free choices, and unfortunately their behavior will have some effect on innocent victims. God does not have to determine who is abusive or who is abused.

The existence of free will and randomness enables individuals to elect to behave badly as a matter of choice. There is a random possibility of involvement with abusive parents, guardians, teachers or priests, for example, where choice is not involved. A bad experience, seemingly inevitable to each of us, is also as possible as an undeserved favorable circumstance. Understanding that bad choices will probably be made and that both good and bad circumstances will be encountered seems inevitable. God's love and support enables us to deal with good and bad fortune and good and bad decisions with some degree of equanimity. Hopefully our experiences allow us to learn how to improve our own behavior as well as provide support and assistance to others.

We have considered that creation might be stable and infinite, with individual life unending in a single form. Or it might be temporal and dynamic, continually evolving until the moment of its expiration. When I was fortyfive, I would have opted for the stable and infinite. Now at the age of seventy-five I have had a heart attack that required resuscitation, kidney stones, hip replacements, a knee replacement, lumbar fusion, cancer, and a recurrence of that cancer. Currently I am dealing with issues related to additional back surgery. Yet, I am active, in generally good health, and physically strong. My point is we are not immortal, and we know it. What we do not know are the details of our departure and our circumstances after death. I love this existence, yet I look forward to transitioning to another possibility when it is over. I also view the end of this life differently than I did at forty-five. I do not want to be Methuselah. Nine hundred years would be a sentence, not an opportunity. While I am not ready to accept termination without a battle, I view death very differently than I did twenty years ago or earlier. "To everything there is a season . . ."

My God is here with me while I deal with being an individual, the member of a family, the member of a community, and a fortunate citizen of the United States. My God has never changed, even though everything on His earth changes and continues to evolve. Species become extinct; if we practice poor stewardship, we might bring about our own extinction. Knowledge expanded, particularly after the development of written communication and more recently with the use of computers and electronic networks. Yet my God remains constant and consistent, loving each of us. He supports us without diminishing us and offers succor and assurance in our efforts to do what He has determined will be in our best interests.

BOOK 8

God Is the Answer

Ultimately, we do not justify God. If He exists, He is our reason for being and being the way we are in a world He created. In *The Language of God*, Dr. Francis Collins proposes that God employed evolution as a tool to bring the modern world today into existence. I have no problem accepting that position. In the introduction, I pointed out that the existence of the God of Abraham was a binary circumstance. This chapter will discuss why I believe His existence is supported by logical reasoning and scientific evidence. Two routes can be developed to lead one to a reasonable and logical conclusion. One points out the range of facts and circumstances that support that God exists, while the other analyzes the facts and circumstances employed by those who question or attack His existence.

I have read several of Richard Dawkins's books, including his recent work, *The God Delusion*. He spends considerable time pointing out that the only necessity for our presence on the earth was a few billion years of relative stability and a primordial soup of chemicals and electrical disturbances. In *The Selfish Gene*, Dawkins goes to some lengths to illustrate how our genetic composition is exclusively responsible for our intellectual and emotional development, including tendencies toward altruism. When looking at a role that God fills in our belief and value systems, Dawkins reduces altruism and love to a genetic source. If that is the case, then C. S. Lewis's argument that all human beings display innate responses to a universal sense of responsibility and concern for others, even to our own detriment, has a basis in genetics and is not proof of a Supreme Being. Dawkins stretches believability, even using game theory and cost-benefit analysis to make his point. It is difficult, however, to reconcile a system built upon survival of the fittest with altruism and love, the prime message of Christianity:

- Love the Lord your God with all your heart and mind.
- Love your neighbor as yourself.

These two commandments were given as the new covenant. The actions of Christians do not always demonstrate their individual or collective obedience to their own basic tenets, and that is the challenge of redemption. We are all victims of our own free will who are incapable of living up to our own standards, but we are still loved and accepted by our Creator, who gave us His Son to demonstrate His love. On that basis, for more than two thousand years, Christians have given up their lives for their beliefs and to encourage the beliefs of others. It is not credible for selfish genes to give up their own lives for the betterment of others.

Today, some Muslim believers are willing to sacrifice their lives for a jihad that, in their minds, attacks heretical beliefs and accepts self-sacrifice while destroying the lives of infidels. In the 1930s and 1940s, Nazis murdered Jews to fulfill their own doctrine of Aryan superiority and racial purity. Christians by the thousands, hundreds of thousands, and millions have sacrificed themselves while trying to teach love and faith to others. I cannot reconcile natural selection with the martyrdom of early Christians or the modern sacrifice of missionaries in remote corners of the earth or within our own urban jungles. Jihad is a cost-benefit approach that relies on killing more infidels than martyrs. Genocide is the ultimate promotion of self-interest through the slaughter of others. The concept of altruistic Christian sacrifice is self-sacrifice for the benefit of others: "Greater love hath no man but that he lay down his life for others."

Atheists equate altruism and love as lust, group hypnosis, long-term selfinterest, or some other factor that forces compliance with a predetermined pattern of behavior whether directly or subconsciously. Sacrifice without expectation of reward is inconsistent with natural selection or survival of the fittest. The scientific reality of evolution is not, however, antithetical with realities of love and affection as supported and encouraged by a benevolent God.

Those who rely on accident, genetics, and natural selection have a problem rationalizing the concept of the better self. It is true that not everyone who strives to improve himself is able to consistently live the selfless life and always look to benefit others. Sometimes people's behavior reflects total cynicism and hypocrisy; sometimes their behavior is but a momentary weakness in a pandering environment. None of us seems able to maintain our better self under all circumstances, though there have been shining examples of consistent concern for others. The concept of a better self can be illustrated by providing a better life experience for others, some demonstrable consistency with the "golden rule." The late Randy Pausch, the Carnegie Mellon professor who wrote *The Last Lecture*, is an example of a better self.

I do not know whether he was particularly religious, a Christian, or an atheist. Carl Sagan, probably an agnostic based upon his statement that he saw no scientific evidence of God, certainly exhibited more than a few characteristics of a better self. These men illustrate that it is not essential to be a practicing Christian to demonstrate an example of the better self. However, I believe that a statistical analysis of the best examples of our ability to live up to the concept of the better self would reveal a higher correlation between believing Christians and exemplary behavior than in the non-Christian general population. I believe Christian beliefs and values motivate individuals to emulate, to some extent, the lifestyle and values of the founder of our unique Christian beliefs.

Finally, if the existence of humanity is not a direct result of the plan of a Higher Being—who provides us with insight, values, and experience; enables our higher elements of being, including love, self-sacrifice, and ennobling lives; and who has expectations for our behavior—we are left with only genetics, electro-chemical reactions, and education as influences. I believe this materialistic explanation leads ultimately to the bigoted conclusion that some gene pools are superior to others: natural selection in more primitive environments does not place a higher survival premium on intellect and communication elegance, therefore producing lesser intellectual beings—a basic tenet of fascism and bigotry. While I do not hold that every human being is intellectually, physically, or artistically gifted to the same extent, I also do not see evidence that supports superior ethnic gene pools, a seemingly inevitable conclusion if our existence relied totally on genetics.

The nature of the debate about God's existence does not include any materialist's undeniable evidence that God does not exist. It would indeed diminish our uncertainty if there were a controlled experiment like the one described by Katherine Solomon in Dan Brown's novel *The Lost Symbol* in which the soul could be weighed as it left the body. But such an experiment does not exist in the real world, not now. Science cannot prove the existence of God or the soul in any repeatable physical experiment. We can only apply logic to what we can observe and deduce whether it is more reasonable to conclude that God exists or if we are just, willy-nilly, creatures of an accidental creation.

In his book, *God's Undertaker*, mathematician John C. Lennox reports that in 1916 Professor James H. Leuba surveyed one thousand scientists chosen at random from the 1910 edition of *American Men of Science*. There was a 70 percent response rate: 41.8 percent confirmed their belief in personal immortality and a God who answered prayer; 41.5 percent did not share the belief; and 16.7 percent were agnostic. In 1996, Edward Larson and Larry Witham ran a similar survey, whose results were reported in *Nature*. Their response rate was 60 percent, of which 39.6 percent were believers, 45.5 percent were nonbelievers, and 14.9 percent were agnostic. While other observers drew different conclusions, most were impressed with the consistency over a fifty-year period. Larson and Witham later surveyed the members of the National Academy of Sciences and found that 72.2 percent were atheists, 7 percent were believers, and 20.8 percent identified themselves as agnostics. The results suggest that, today, more eminent scientists are likely to be atheists. I do not know whether it is the skeptical nature of science, the fallibilism approach put forward by Karl Popper, or peer pressure that leads to the inclusion of atheism among the fundamental element of the scientific scholastic community. Unquestionably, materialist scientists, while they cannot find unarguable evidence that points to the absence of God, find comfort in the absence of laboratory proof supporting God's existence. Many scientists find their definition of truth, limited to repeatable physical evidence, sufficient, even as they acknowledge its incompleteness in defining humanity's experience in our physical world.

Lennox goes on to point out that philosopher Sir Alfred North Whitehead's view was "that men became scientific because they expected law in nature, and they expected law in nature because they believed in a lawgiver." This represents the history of science and Christianity; modern science was born and encouraged within the Christian community. Yes, some denominations and even some congregations have been more hostile to science but Christian respect for knowledge dominated over time. Apparently, given the statistics cited above, there was no reciprocity. Most "objective" scientists seem to fear or distrust religion. Perhaps objective scientists and fundamentalist preachers share a reluctance to embrace change and expansion in knowledge and appreciation for God's influence in a dynamic and evolving universe.

There is historical weight to the concept of a Creator since, during most of our time as communicating forms of intelligent life, the vast majority of humanity has embraced the concept. Lennox refers to the myth of a gang of monkeys, each one with a typewriter, producing even a single sonnet by Shakespeare, let alone one of his plays, is improbable enough to be considered impossible. The same statistical argument proves the improbability of producing environments supportive of developing intelligent life as we know it, based upon our experience and scientific knowledge to date. Accidents happen, and in the six billion or so couplings of DNA in our species, we do see evidence of evolutionary change. We do not see evidence of DNA modification on any scale that would produce species origination rather than modification within a species. We cannot connect Homo sapiens and Neanderthal as variants of the same species. We have recently found that most Northern European Homo sapiens have four to six percent Neanderthal DNA encoding indicating evidence of sexual genetic sharing of the two species who shared the same geography for tens of thousands of years.

God is certainly a default answer to the unobservable and improvable mysteries remaining after all scientific avenues have been investigated. I believe that He is the *primary* answer, not an explanation of the gaps. I believe it was Francis Collins who painted the picture of the last physicist climbing the last hill toward complete understanding of the universe who, upon peering over the top, encountered a group of theologians who were wondering why it had taken the scientist so long.

BOOK 9

Faith of Our Fathers

In 1993, my mother died at the age of ninety-six. While I am certainly grateful for any genetic predisposition toward a long life that she bequeathed, I am also greatly impressed by the century of change that she witnessed and coped with in her lifetime. When she was a young girl, Civil War veterans were in their fifties. Local transportation was on horse, by foot, on the occasional bone-crushing bicycle, and long-distance transportation was by steam engine at speeds typically below fifty miles an hour. Lighting at night was by oil lamp and candle. In 1888, Paris had some municipal gas lights but the presence of any lights on township streets was uncommon in the American Midwest. Around the turn of the century the United States, while a growing manufacturing nation, was still an agrarian society.

Two of America's greatest inventor/industrialists were in their fifties in 1897, the year my mother was born: George Westinghouse and Thomas Edison. In 1895, Westinghouse "electrified" the city of Buffalo using AC power transmitted from Niagara Falls. By 1905, the combination of air brakes and electrical transmission, resulting from innovations born of the efforts of both men, led to elevated trains in parts of New York City. According to my mother, she was fourteen when her mother went to an auto dealer, bought a car, and told her to drive them all home. This was in Galion, Ohio. In July 1969, almost sixty years later, Mom watched on television as Neil Armstrong walked on the moon. Since 1960, one of her sons has participated in the computer industry. Television, radio, automobiles, airplanes, movies, computers, biological weapons, modern pharmacology, and two World Wars are among the modern phenomena that she encountered.

Some sixty years before my mother's birth, Mary Baker Eddy (1821–1910) was born in the northeast United States. In 1879, she founded a religion called Christian Science though she was certainly not a scientist and some would argue that, in spite of her Congregationalist upbringing, she was not a conventional Christian theologian. However, during the Victorian period of male supremacy, she established a lasting religious movement. Her theories of anti-materialism embodied in the "Scientific Statement of Being," do not square with modern genetics, physics, or biology. She believed in the potential spiritual perfection of all humans, identified a Christ existence in each of us, and believed that we possess qualities that traditional theology restricts solely to the Son of God. What is significant, in my opinion, is that she developed a new theology that expanded traditional dogma and theology to include experience that was not available to the original writers of the Bible. But she did not refute that the Bible reflected the Word of God and contained truth.

I am not a Christian Scientist, although I attended that church in my youth while also singing in the local Episcopal boys' choir. My point is that Christian Science theology was the response of a devout individual and her many followers to their interpretation of the real world. I find gaps in a denial of materiality that seeks to limit my appreciation of all of God's creation. I find it more acceptable to consider that any creation of a dynamic and infinite universe must contain elements of randomness, dialecticism, and individual free will, all of which can be in contention for control at any time. Only the concept of timelessness can resolve transient individual misfortune into a dimension in which the greatest good can be realized. Humans thrive on our ability to respond to challenges. A steady state of satisfaction (i.e., heaven) would ultimately not provide any sense of self-fulfillment or self-satisfaction.

I believe that religion, our core of beliefs about our relationship to God, changes over time as we come to appreciate more of the miracle of the universe in which we live. Religion and science both continuously try to delve into the mysteries of our being, our purpose, and our relationships to each other, our created world, and our Creator. If that Creator were only accident and natural selection that would leave a lot of issues to resolve, specifically the nontangible, nonmaterialistic components of our existence and experience.

I must emphasize that in my seventy-five years on this earth, I have been a pragmatic, hi-tech businessman who is familiar with Sarbanes-Oxley and the opinions of the Financial Accounting Standards Board. These are daily issues of business practice. When I began to read the viewpoints of Owen Gingerich, John Polkinghorne, Francis Collins, and Darrel Falk on the relationship of science and religion, I felt as though my training, vocabulary, and prior experience were inadequate for the task. Nevertheless, I am compelled to provide an aging layman's outlook on these complex subjects.

My God of today is the God of Abraham, Isaac, and Moses as well as the God of the New Covenant. He is the same God we currently worship and relate to personally in this era of cosmology and quantum mechanics. God does not change, but our perception of Him has certainly changed since His initial encounters with members of the tribes of Israel as recorded in the Torah. I appreciate that there are religious communities that do not employ electricity, gasoline motors, or other modern conveniences as they pursue their agrarian lifestyles in today's modern world. This denial of modern advantages, which most of us perceive as current reality, is their right. But while they may thrive economically as the value of farm products increases internationally, they do constitute an ever decreasing percentage of our total population. Also, many of them have modified their religious restrictions and observations to accommodate changes spurred by their encounters with neighboring societies, agricultural science, economic reality, and regulatory requirements for providing components of our food supply. I do not criticize this accommodation as a loss of principle. Rather, it is recognition that conditions have changed and consequentially differences, even slight ones, have been grudgingly accepted. Even the most conservative adherents among us modify their perception of God when faced with the encroaching reality of the world they try to not accept.

Practicing Christians who accept scientific realities, including stem-cell potential; the multiple problems caused by technology; and the current potential for atomic, biological, or chemical annihilation are responsible Christians who are trying to achieve the potential that God provided us. They employ love as the primary vehicle for accomplishing God's will. Christians who practice more doctrinaire and restrictive religious observances also have the right to identify themselves as practicing Christians, although I have trouble reconciling their God-limiting practices and rituals with the liberating theology of the Son of God. This illustrates the point made by John Polkinghorne in *Quantum Physics and Theology*: that building scientific knowledge is a more linear process that consists of gathering observations. Theology is a more complex diachronic process that includes experience, knowledge of the world, as well as revelation, and faith in other possibilities.

Scientific knowledge expands linearly over time, which enhances its credibility to some. This linear extension occurs particularly as the newly expanded reality is illustrated in repeatable laboratory experiments. Our religious knowledge and enlightenment expands through shared experience, shared intuition, and revelation. Karl Popper's term fallibilism, used to enhance scientific credibility, holds that while science hypothesizes and then seeks the singular negative to reject the hypothesis, the humanities expand the hypothesis to encompass the exception when it occurs. This expansion can continue to propound the adjusted hypothetical fable as truth. There are several examples in science in which observed phenomena are extrapolated into a general theory despite the single observation necessary to challenge validity. For example, while genetic adjustments have been observed and repeated, natural selection alone does not explain the irreducible complexity of single-celled creatures not traceable to a slowly evolving modification. Similarly, the Cambrian explosion of new species that occurred about 530 million years ago, a period that is equivalent to about 10 percent of the life of our planet, does not seem consistent with the concept of species slowly evolving from a mythical tree of life. Fallibilism therefore does not seem to apply to post-Newtonian science in biology, cosmology, or physics when the hypothesis has not been reduced to observed and repeatable truth.

Single-event fallibilism, as a test of truth, is in contrast to Polkinghorne's work in *Quantum Physics and Theology*, which illustrates the parallels between science and religion. Polkinghorne writes, "The God of truth will not be a deceiver, and insight into the divine character, manifested either in the works of creation or in the events of revelation, can be relied upon not to mislead." His position also suggests the expansion of understanding over time in both religion and science. He is not saying that there is new truth but that we discover truth in expanding experience and understanding.

When viewing today's Christian beliefs versus those of two hundred years ago, one will encounter many modifications in each of the various denominations, including the Latter Day Saints. The Roman Catholic Church employs a litany of the Mass in the language of the country in which it resides. In the musical *The Book of Mormon*, the lyric in one song points out that in 1978, I believe it was, God changed His opinion about black people. Most Methodists today do not consider dancing to be the devil's tool. Most Presbyterians do not follow John Calvin's doctrine of predestination. Modification comes to all belief systems albeit sometimes very slowly.

BOOK 10

Agnosticism and Atheism

While this book is about reconciliation between science and faith, I must acknowledge that many accomplished, intelligent scientists have promoted agnosticism and frequently atheism. Before examining their viewpoints, I think it will be worthwhile to spend a brief time on semantics. Religion, as I have used it in this book, includes the practices of worship, organization, and ritual observed by various sects, denominations, and congregations. Each religion is defined by its theology, which establishes the rationale and history of its practices. Theology is established, defended, and occasionally modified by authorized representatives—the clergy—of each sect, denomination, or congregation or by a denominational assembly. Faith is the belief that is accepted and practiced by individual members of a denomination, sect, or congregation. The religion, theology, and clergy of a congregation, sect, or denomination may be presenting a dogma that is not observed as faith by the believers. I know many devout Roman Catholics, for example, whose personal faith does not accept papal direction on the issue of birth control. I also accept that the faith of individuals can strengthen and uphold a theological position or weaken that position when that faith does not conform to institutional theology.

The point of these distinctions is to explain how a religion may develop a theology and practices that are inconsistent with the precepts that undergird the faith of its believers. Furthermore, many actions that have been performed in the name of religion had nothing to do with the faith that Jesus, Mohammad, or other leaders of faith preached or practiced. With this as background, I found it valuable to reflect on the positions expressed by Richard Dawkins, Christopher Hitchens, Sam Harris, et al., and to compare those ideas to the concepts of C. S. Lewis, Francis Collins, Darrel Falk, Owen Gingerich, and Antony Flew. In the following discussion, I am sure I will oversimplify some positions and omit significant nuances or sophisticated elements of debate. However, I am attempting to develop my own position in the hope that some might find it helpful or encouraging.

Value of the Word

I have found that most atheists, particularly scientific atheists, look to the scriptures as they would look to the laws of physics when attempting to define the religion that is being evaluated or debated. Dawkins, Hitchens, and Harris, for example, all base a great deal of their criticism of religion on the literal interpretation of stories in Holy Text. These authors depict God as a killer or sadist in Old Testament stories; God employing vengeance to encourage belief; and God rejecting some, if not most of his creatures, and excluding them from His redemption as reasons for rejecting a less than friendly Creator. These points are employed whether the authors are considering Islam, Buddhism, Hinduism, or Christianity.

I am not trying to defend all religious belief in this treatise, so my response will be limited to my observations of the Bible and Christianity. In my opinion, the Bible was written and translated by men, although I believe the authors and translators were individually inspired by God. I am aware that many of the books of the Old Testament were passed on orally for thousands of years before people learned how to write. I am aware of the inherent unreliability of eyewitnesses even in current system of legal jurisprudence. I have read translations of Gnostic texts that vary greatly from the traditional scripture stories of the Bible since the time of Saint Jerome. The entire Bible was written when people believed the earth was flat and at the center of the universe, that the sun and stars circled the earth. Today people know that the earth is spherical and orbits the sun, and that the sun is one of several billion or so stars in the Milky Way galaxy, which in turn is one of more than many billions of galaxies. I also believe that man has been wrestling over how he relates to God, his fellow man, and even to himself, since he first qualified as an intelligent being.

I have read several texts translated and preserved from the Renaissance, Reformation, the Age of Enlightenment, and other periods of history. Historical fiction and nonfiction from those eras do reflect the truth, though perhaps not what we now know about our relative place in the universe and the scale of creation. The Bible contains identified parables, one of the primary teaching devices employed by Jesus, as well as allegorical tales and other methods that are subject to interpretation by the reader. The Bible has truth at its core, and it is the task of the believer to understand and seek what is contained within it.

Evil Has Been Performed in the Name of Religion

The clergy, theology, and religion are institutions or processes of man that are supposed to be consistent with his faith. Pedophile priests, torturing inquisitors, Cromwell's destroyers of idolatry, and holy armies represent human frailty and are not weaknesses of the faith. People who conduct evil in the name of religion have all of the character flaws inherent to our species. This is the two-edged sword of free will. Our decision to do what is right versus what may be more convenient or easier—when we follow God's instruction to love Him and our neighbor—is part of what gives us value to our Creator. Free will requires our ability to do evil or dumb things or conversely to always consider our own long-term best interests.

PHILIP S. RADCLIFFE

There Is No Evidence to Prove the Existence of God

Based on the criteria of objective materialism, this observation has an element of truth about it. However, not all reality is represented by objective materialism. Even the esteemed atheist Sam Harris acknowledges, in *The End of Faith*, that:

> The claims of mystics are neurologically quite astute. No human being has ever experienced an objective world or even a world at all. You are at this moment, having a visionary experience. The world that you see or hear is nothing more than a modification of your consciousness, the physical status of which remains a mystery.

He goes on to point out that sensory perception is edited by our consciousness and, even more significantly, for every neuron that receives an external stimulus there are ten to a hundred that are "talking" to each other and ultimately transferring thought to our frontal lobe, where our restrainers temper what we present as thought. If God exists, He is metaphysical or beyond physics, and our evidence is logic, revelation, and reason, not objective presence.

A Creator God Would Have Engineered a Better System

From the relatively minor consideration that an all-knowing God would never have given us an appendix to the wrenching truth that the death of a beloved child is not viewed as consistent with the design of a loving God, His design has been criticized. These and other examples are presented relative to the flaws in God's design, promoting the ultimate conclusion that our existence is happenstance. Every one of us has, at one time or another, imagined our own Eden. I would venture the opinion that if our individual Eden was realized, it would not satisfy even our own selves for more than a brief period of time. If my previous observations are at least substantially correct, God's design for us includes competition, a sense of the dialectic, a component of randomness, and individual free will. These components account for the death of innocents, destructive storms, disease, and random natural disasters. Our own character flaws, as emphasized through free will, create repression, war, and injustice. The alternative is some form of preplanned existence with a concurrent loss of independence and mutual respect. Think about an Eden that is still temporal for all inhabitants; how do you introduce death except randomly?

In contrast, consider our universe as we have come to know and appreciate it. The activities now in progress at the LHC site near Geneva, Switzerland, will reveal more information at the subatomic level about what differentiates energy and mass in terms of composition and transition. This is the stuff of which the big bang was made. Whatever is revealed, you can be assured the process will introduce more new questions. From this level of minute detail up to the death of stars creating the heavy elements required for life on earth, the amazing combination of physical elements and activities that support our existence had an extremely remote probability of ever occurring. Yet here we are, aware of our own existence and temporal reality. You design a superior system that occurs in an instant and supports our life forms 14.5 billion years later with the possibility that there are others like us among the billions of billions of stars. I do not accept that the presence of my appendix reflects negatively on God's design abilities. This is divine design, but not Young Earth Creationism. Humans have accomplished some truly amazing engineering accomplishments, but our intellect, compared to that required to accomplish creation and support intelligent life, is severely limited. Any suggestion of possible improvements upon that creation reflects unbelievable arrogance.

A Syllogistic Approach to Atheism

Sam Harris, a well-known American atheist, has developed a syllogistic approach in his argument against belief in any god. In *The End of Faith*, he incorporates many of the points discussed previously, but wraps them in a framework of logic that bears consideration.

Harris says that since most neural activity occurs between neurons not directly involved with sensory information, it follows that this network is dealing with internal ideas and beliefs. Therefore, belief and faith are extremely important as precursors to actions. As we believe, so we shall act. Illogical, unproven, and unreasonable religious faith, whether Christian, Jewish, Muslim, or any other faith-based belief, leads irrevocably to illogical and unreasonable acts and impedes reasoned analysis of true ethical and moral behavior. Furthermore, unproven belief is not a reliable basis for intellectual exchanges between humans, particularly those who embody different faiths. Ergo, people should accept, as a basis for their beliefs, only those concepts that can be validated by some scientific method.

This seems a reasoned approach until you get to the basics of what can be observed via the scientific method and what is considered illogical or unreasonable and according to what set of standards. Here, Harris seems to rely on the Word as the sole expression of truth in religion. He goes to great length to explain why Islam, based upon the Koran, is repressive, violent, and dangerous, and I must say that his case seems irrefutable, given the behavior of some Muslims before and since September 11, 2001. However, I am a Christian who looks at the Bible as a text that reveals truth about redemption and our relationship with God, within the context of the scientific knowledge and cultural influence that was present during biblical and later times. As such, I dismiss some of the incongruities and severe practices of the scriptural writers, on the basis of then-contemporary understanding. Abraham's willingness to sacrifice his son was a story told about the value of fidelity to God, not a warning about child abuse. Religions at that point had practiced animal and human sacrifice as acceptable rituals so their use in a story to illustrate a different point can be accepted as license by the storyteller whether or not it actually happened. The story also was passed on for thousands of years before it was written down. If the Word of the Bible is accepted as valid within the context of the cultures and worldly knowledge of the period in which it was first told or written down, we can identify within it reasoned and logical support for loving, tolerant, and steadfast behavior toward all who share our universe, both known and as yet unknown.

The "scientific method" involves three elements for acceptability: test, observe, and repeat. However, not all scientific knowledge meets this rigorous demand. Science employs statistics to indicate empirical conditions, but the resulting "facts" are not laws of nature. Newtonian physics have met all requirements of the method many times and still do in many physics labs. It takes a complete change of scale to prove that these previously observed facts do not always represent the whole truth. Objective, critical, or skeptical materialism cannot prove truth beyond physical presence or absence. Logic and reason still yield truth to be unassailable by science. I agree with Harris that the Bible interpreted literally is neither objectively true nor logical or reasonable. That does not mean that the Bible is not true when viewed as a whole, in the context of its historical period and given reasonable interpretation to accommodate the societal norms when it was written.

Harris holds that existence includes awareness of self and others. He also points out that awareness of "I" incorporates more than a physical, chemical, or biologic presence. For example, a man can recognize his own hand as a part of himself that contains DNA, nerves, and blood. Yet he also is aware if his hand were removed, he would still have self and awareness. Ultimately, Harris seems to opt for secular meditation as a vehicle to acknowledge self and promoting broad support for a concept akin to the Golden Rule in order to experience satisfaction in self and happiness in others. These, rather than dogmatic faith, seem to be his criteria for ethical, reasoned behavior.

My problem with Harris is his rejection of reason and curiosity as fundamental parts of faith. C. S. Lewis did not come to his acceptance of faith during an emotional revelation on his personal road to Damascus. Most intelligent modern believers interpret the scriptures as guides to behavior among peers, illustrations for maintenance of healthy relationships, and conformity with God's primary principles without requiring literal acceptance of every jot and title either as originally written or modified by several translators.

God gave us the gifts of questioning his holy orders to differentiate between glibness and sincere reasoned conduct. We do not always practice righteous skepticism with discipline and analysis. "What Would Jesus Do?" is a legitimate question, but the answer is not always apparent and obvious. A better question is, why do you really care? Individual motivation is not biological, objectively verifiable, or even consistent.

The breadth of Harris's consideration does induce greater respect than does the work of either Richard Dawkins or Christopher Hitchens, primarily because Harris acknowledges that there is empirical and revealed evidence of life or the soul beyond pure material existence. In *The End of Faith*, he includes the innate desire to share happiness and satisfaction with others in terms of romance, friendship, or charity as elements of living. His criticism is of what he finds to be intolerable: unreasoned faith and dogmatic justification. In contrast, Dawkins goes to great length to show that all aspects of intelligent life owe their existence to the survival of selfish genes and nothing more. In *God Is Not Great*, Christopher Hitchens employs the journalist's anecdotal approach, selecting circumstances to illustrate his point that "religion poisons everything," the book's subtitle. Hitchens never acknowledges that religion has also accomplished great, positive, and lifesaving programs, in both large-scale projects and individual events, such as recovery from addiction via twelve-step programs. I found Hitchens's analysis to be a case-by-case discussion of cause and effect without any indepth questioning of the positive impact religion has had on human experience, though he frequently points out where religion has led to negative outcomes.

The criticisms leveled by atheists or agnostics need to be evaluated by those who advocate for any religious belief. I have not heard a strong defense of human rights, giving consideration to gender; religious tolerance; and sexual preference by any Muslim clerics. If Islamic religious practices cannot accommodate universal acceptance of the human condition in all of its diversity, they are inconsistent with any understanding I have of God. I have similar difficulty with unreasoned dogma practiced by any so-called Christian sect that similarly justifies unchristian behavior by citing literal quotations or offers a narrow and discriminatory interpretation of the Holy Text.

This position is not meant to limit discussion of Christian positions on issues such as birth control, abortion, homosexual clerics, or stem-cell ethics. There are moral and ethical positions over which believers within the family of Christians can disagree. Over time, many of these issues will be resolved to a single acceptable solution. As an example, if homosexuality is only caused as a genetic condition, then there is no danger that homosexuals will "recruit" impressionable youth to their lifestyle. If, on the other hand, the appeal of a role-model cleric, teacher, or youth leader can be modeled to youth who are influenced by adults in positions of authority, I believe social institutions have a right to defend their ethical positions by refusing to recruit adherents of what some would call deviant behavior. I am not convinced that gay people can, or desire to, recruit straight people. In the more than forty years since Neil Armstrong took his "small step for a man" on the moon, the population of the earth has doubled. This fact will have direct bearing on humanity's ethical evaluation of issues related to birth control and abortion. Remembering always to love our God and treat our neighbors as we would wish to be treated are conditions we should impose on all our ethical dilemmas.

BOOK 11

A Layman's View

I have always enjoyed reading. For many years, I have read biographies, action novels, and historical novels. Michael Crichton was my favorite author. I appreciated the authority his background as a physician provided him in areas of scientific exposition. I also enjoyed my subscription to *Scientific American* for many years. My occupation required reading technical tracts and manuals as well as legal and accounting material. When my career reading requirements slowed down, I played more golf. Then around 2000, my son gave me *The Elegant Universe* by Brian Greene. This introduction to quantum mechanics and string theory whet my appetite to pursue a broader range of literature addressing our presence in the universe and the mechanics of how the universe works, viewed through the lens of critical realism and metaphysics. A near-death experience in January 2001 provided me with more incentive to examine the great issues of why we are here and why things are as they are.

I started my next level of exploration with two books by Jared Diamond: *Guns, Germs, and Steel* and *Collapse*. I revisited C. S. Lewis's *Mere Christianity* and several of Bart D. Ehrman's expositions on Bible history. Then, I was off into a world of nonfiction, including most all of C. S. Lewis's works on theology and those by several other authors cited earlier in this book. I still maintained some level of recreational reading but my appreciation of more intellectually challenging nonfiction grew exponentially. This inspired me to start writing, beginning with a collection of journals that I subsequently organized by topic into a memoir. It defined many of my values based on my experiences and reading up to that point. Meanwhile, I continued reading more works written by scientists and academicians with an occasional theologian in the mix. I found the values and opinions I had formed based upon my reasoning and experience often were expressed more elegantly and in a more academic fashion by many of those authors.

It was sometimes difficult to recollect which came first—my independent reasoned conclusion or the supporting or contrary conclusions expressed by others. As John Polkinghorne expressed, my exercise in testing my conclusions based on my readings, reasoning, experience, and revelation has at least a cousinly relationship to the methodology of critical realism. My driving force in expressing my conclusions is twofold: First, such an exercise always helps an author clarify his own experience into a logical whole. Second, much of the material I have read is presented in an academic way, and I wanted to take a less formal approach. The academic format is appropriate for review by other experts, scientists, and academicians. I have been a pragmatic businessman for most of my life. I represent most reasonably well-educated, aging, middle-class Americans. While I do not present my conclusions as theology, a majority view among my socioeconomic class, or a scientific discourse supporting my hypotheses, I believe I reflect conclusions that an informed layman can understand. This layman's exposition might help more professional opinion shapers to see how some of their works are being interpreted or misinterpreted by at least some of their readers, assuming my conclusions are representative.

My first effort at presenting my conclusions was to discuss the unification between science and religion. Works that illustrate a scientific view that relies on critical realism and materialism and do not account for metaphysical forces are as close-minded and stubborn as religion that tries to deny provable scientific fact. Neither approach to our world and the stewardship of the earth has much hope of arriving at valid solutions for our continued existence. Looking into the history of the interaction between science and religion, one immediately encounters the extended differences between the Catholic Church and the astronomy of Copernicus (1473–1543) and Galileo (1564–1642) and also the differences with the Protestant community and Johannes Kepler (1571–1630). Kepler wrote, "Praise and celebrate with me the wisdom and magnitude of the Creator, which I lay open before you by means of a deeper explanation of the structure of the world, by the search for its causes." Today, even the literal tradition of Bible interpretation accepts that the earth is round, the sun is at the center of our solar system, and the universe has multiple galaxies.

The Bible is not only nonfiction literature; it is Holy Scripture and reflects eternal truth. It is constantly amazing to me that I can read words in a twothousand—to four-thousand-year-old text and gain insight into my actions today. The Bible is the Word of God delivered to us within the limits of our culture and our contemporary ability to comprehend, a moving target. The reformer John Wesley (1703–1791) described the book of Genesis as follows: "The inspired penman in this history wrote for the Jews first and, calculating his narratives for the infant state of the church, described things by their outward sensible appearance, and leaves us, by further discoveries of the divine light, to be led into the understanding of the mysteries couched under them." Later he wrote about Genesis 1:3: "He made the stars also— which were spoken of only in general, for the scriptures were written not to gratify our curiosity but to lead us to God." If we accept that we were created with curiosity and therefore seek knowledge as a gift from God, the expansion of scientific knowledge is not anti-religious but consistent with God's creation. Similarly, when literal interpretation of a biblical passage conflicts with scientific fact, it may merely reflect the limitations of the scriptural author and not religion's anti-scientific bias. The Bible is neither inerrant in terms of physical explanations nor complete in its description of literal history or even the complete text of Jesus's sayings and biography. The closing chapter of John states that the disciple saw these things that he recorded, but he supposes that if all things that Jesus did were written down, the world could not contain the books. This sentiment seems to acknowledge that not each word of the Bible has to be consistent with material fact to represent eternal truth.

Jared Diamond uses the terms "proximate cause" and "ultimate cause" to discriminate between a physical event and the underlying physical, metaphysical, sociological, or psychological causes that give rise to the event. For example, the populations of Easter Island apparently fell into conflict over diminishing food supplies and either killed each other off or starved to death. The proximate cause of societal collapse was conflict and starvation; the ultimate cause was deforestation, which reduced the availability of tillable land and thus the food supply. In his 2005 William Belden Noble Lecture at Harvard, Owen Gingerich used the terms "efficient cause" and "final cause" to distinguish between how things work (efficient) and why things work that way (final). According to Gingerich, science is "a neutral way of explaining *how* things *work*, not anti God or Atheistic" (emphasis mine). He points out that when science becomes a materialist philosophy that explains why things work, it becomes an ideology that raises science to the rank of final cause. For example, he notes, "it is just as wrong to present evolution in high school classrooms as a final cause as it is to fob off Intelligent Design as a substitute for efficacious efficient cause." He differentiates the creationist Intelligent Design from an intelligent design that was employed by the Creator and includes the process of evolution.

Science and mathematics deal with the efficient cause that leads to the creation of matter and energy. Religion and philosophy deal with the issues of the ultimate cause. Both areas of intellectual exercise seek truth, and historically, if one area ignores the truth as revealed by the methods appropriately employed by the other, its credibility is diminished in its own field. Philosophy and religion that ignore the reality demonstrated by science require greater adherence to dogma and look less to reason. Science that diminishes the truth of philosophy and religion encounters the danger of substituting equations for ethical values and context.

BOOK 12

A New View of the Evidence

I have recently finished reading some new books on the subjects of the existence of the Creator and the relationship of science to religious faith. One is *The Big Questions in Science and Religion* by Keith Ward; another is *The Case for a Creator* by Lee Strobel; and a third is *The Devil's Delusion* by David Berlinski. Ward is an illustrious Oxford don who holds a philosophy chair and is also an ordained Anglican priest. Strobel is a journalist who has written several books on contemporary religion. David Berlinski has a PhD from Princeton, University, has taught mathematics, and wrote *A Tour of the Calculus*, among other works. These brief biographical comments do not do justice to any of the aforementioned authors but serve to indicate the different approaches each one employs while examining the existence of a Supreme Being and reconciling intelligent design with skeptical materialism.

While the writing style and technique of evidentiary review among these works are very different, I believe it is a fair conclusion to state that never in the history of mankind has there been more scientific evidence to support the conclusion that our universe was created as the result of a plan to create selfaware, intelligent life. Ward approaches this subject from a more philosophical point of view, while Strobel employs the journalistic technique of interviewing

A SHOTGUN WEDDING

qualified scientific experts. Berlinski's book has been called a "work of learned polemical writing [that] excoriates its (science's) atheist pretensions from within."

Ward is a recognized authority on comparative religions and philosophy. He puts current scientific discoveries in the context of a growing conclusion that science supports rather than refutes the existence of a Supreme Creator. Strobel takes a more evidentiary review and illustrates, through the responses of his interviewees, how science that follows the evidence indicates that we are the result of a planned creation. Berlinski firmly plants his tongue in his cheek and deflates science for its pomposity, among other shortcomings. As an example, after reviewing the history and development of the Standard Model, including the Yang-Mills theory of the 1960s and the work of Gross, Politzer and Wilczek in the 1970s, he writes:

> If the Standard Model is a triumph, [it] is not one that is unalloyed. The Standard Model cannot explain the transition from the elementary particles to states of matter in which the elementary particles are bound to one another and so form complex structures. It is in this sense incomplete.
>
> The Standard Model is not only incomplete but arbitrary. Like any physical theory, it contains at least twenty-one numerical parameters that designate specific properties. These cannot be derived from the theory. Physicists are in the position of a master couturier who has to allow one of his finest creations to appear on the runway with its basting lines and tacking pins still affixed.

Strobel interviews qualified experts such as Johnathan Wells, Robin Collins, Jay Wesley Richards, Guillermo Gonzalez, Michael Behe, Stephen Meyer, William Lane Craig, and J. P. Moreland. Collectively, these gentlemen can be characterized as PhDs; many are still in academe, while others are published authorities. Their areas of expertise include molecular biology, chemistry, biochemistry, astronomy, physics, philosophy, and theology. Strobel is an unapologetic believer and writes most of the material for the Willow Creek Association, which represents itself as a nondenominational and presumably evangelistic organization that provides materials and training sessions to help member churches convert the nonbelieving.

These three authors demonstrate three of the approaches that can be employed to reconcile scientific evidence and reason in support of the existence of a Supreme Being. The interview approach runs the risk of being anecdotal and perhaps may bypass facts not mentioned by the interviewees. The philosophical approach can degenerate into a rejection of physical evidence in favor of pure metaphysical reasoning. A scientific analysis may reflect a personal bias. These authors use techniques and experience to ameliorate any individual tendency to slip into logical traps that would reduce the efficacy of their presentations. For example, Strobel, in addition to the several expert witnesses he interviews, cites information from additional sources that both supports and attacks the conclusions of his experts, and uses this material to frame his interview questions. Berlinski, a nonpracticing Jew who is still a believer in God, segregates his discussion into various disciplines and then covers each area, lobbing his verbal hooks after giving full disclosure to the argument. Ward uses a more philosophical approach; he presents points of view and enables readers to select their own conclusions, while subtly commenting that the most reasonable readers seem to pick the most reasonable solutions.

In my experience, even different individuals from the same gene pool and raised in the same environment experience life and individual events uniquely. Thus different approaches examining the source of creation will arrive at their individual conclusions by examining the evidence and using logical steps. There are times when I believe that a weakness of the arguments supporting the existence of God is their variety of evidence and points of debate. Atheistic arguments seem more repetitive and, to my eyes and ears, retell sophomoric complaints about how life treats us.

BOOK 13

Epilogue: There Is a God

Antony Flew (1923–2010), once a diehard atheist, wrote *There Is a God*, whose title I use to name this chapter. Perhaps I had a subconscious desire to conclude this part of my book with a positive reinforcement of my beliefs, or perhaps Flew's book represents the closest summary of truth that I have recently encountered. Flew promoted himself on his book cover as "the world's most notorious atheist," and the book relates how he changed his mind. Some of his former colleagues pointed out that at age of eighty he accepted Pascal's Wager rather than take a chance with his eternal soul. I, however, don't believe that fear of an unknown eternity held much weight with Flew.

Recent scientific discoveries led to his logical conclusion that God does exist and that He created our universe not only to be compatible with life but to encourage the development and advancement of intelligent life. As I read Flew's presentation and recalled the points of others such as C. S. Lewis, Francis Collins, Owen Gingerich, and Darrel Falk, it reinforced my own conviction, based on the physical and logical evidence as I interpreted it. Individual scientists cannot prove the negative, and the data actually support the existence of creative intelligence in the universe. *The Mind of God* by Paul Davies more than reinforces Flew's conclusion that

> The physical species Homo may count for nothing, but the existence of mind in some organism on some planet in the universe is surely a fact of fundamental significance. Through conscious beings the universe has generated self-awareness. This can be no trivial detail, no minor byproduct of mindless, purposeless forces. We are truly meant to be here.

In the introduction, I stated that I was writing to my fellow occupants in the pews on Sunday mornings. I noted, based on what I've read, that the number of people attending mainline Christian churches has declined and continues to decline. As I read Karen Armstrong's *The Case for God* and Paul Davies's *The Mind of God*, I wonder if the homilies and prayers offered by clergy might be part of the issue. Armstrong states that the reason for belief and its ultimate value to humanity is that it addresses the challenges of the nonphysical world, including grief, pain, and sorrow. In contrast, Davies examines the rational basis for knowing that we are in a creation that was designed for us and continues to grow and develop, including the possible birth of new universes from within black holes in this one. My point is not that all of my fellow congregants need physics lectures on cosmology and theoretical physics. But neither do all of us need inflexible, lectionary-driven discourse on the interpretation of biblical text with limited reflection on the impact the Creator has on our living world, including all of the new dimensions of scientific understanding. Albert Einstein once said, "The only incomprehensible thing about our universe is that it is comprehensible." It seems to me that our world is infinitely more comprehensible to accomplished scientists who are also religious thinkers. Perhaps this observation moved the renowned astronomer Sir Fred Hoyle to remark, "I have always thought it curious that, while most scientists claim to eschew religion, it actually dominates their thoughts more than it does the clergy."

Once we acknowledge God's existence, we can address the issues of our relationship with Him and His admonitions on our conduct in His creation. The three major monotheistic religions—Judaism, Christianity, and Islam— are all joined in the common root of Abraham and the Old Testament. As I previously commented, I find it credible that the writers of the Old Testament and the stories they related were inspired by God but reflected the knowledge and culture of their time. Based on my reading and interpretation, when reading the Old Testament, I am not terribly involved in the importance of lineage except as it affected a particular character's bona fides and therefore provided some insight into their point of narration. I am not concerned whether or not the walls of Jericho tumbled down just after trumpets were sounded. I am more concerned with the spiritual message that story tries to evoke. I know in my experience that when teammates retell particular events about our undefeated high-school football season there will be some inconsistency and mentions of individual glory that not all of us recall in exactly the same detail. However, we did not lose a game, and we did not have the same degree of physical talent that many of our opponents did. Our accomplishments were real, and they provide a lesson in how preparation, dedication, motivation, and teamwork can achieve results beyond the sum of the available talent. I heard a sermon once that stated perhaps the lesson of Jericho is to take risks for righteous purpose, as Rahab did when she housed Joshua's spies.

The New Testament was written fifty to one hundred years after the events of Jesus's life. Nevertheless, there were other contemporaneous accounts in Roman journals and governmental records that provide some substantiation of the narrative of the Gospels. There was not a 24/7 news channel that could record all the events of the day, but there were five thousand witnesses to the miracle of the loaves and fishes. (Actually only males were counted, so the probable attendance was something in excess of ten thousand, when women and children are included.) There were also witnesses at the Crucifixion, the Sermon on the Mount, and other events, any of whom would have corrected accounts that appeared in texts at early churches. Moreover, the history of the early Christian church includes competitive and even antagonistic denominations that anxiously sought to discredit the Christians and their text as it developed. Most certainly, witnesses to discredit the miracles and other demonstrations of faith would have been sought out and well rewarded to diminish or destroy this growing and governmentally or politically uncontrolled movement. It is also reasonably and logically consistent that a Creator God, having a desire not to employ His will over His intelligent beings, would have employed vehicles, including prophets and even His own Son, to reinforce His message to His creation.

By contrast, the message of the Koran was recorded by Muhammad's daughter and son-in-law as a series of multiline stanzas dictated by the illiterate prophet. The stanzas are in a poetic form rather than as narrative prose. The message was originally designed to develop a national unity, supported by arms, to develop an Arab nation. The nationalist fervor extended even when other states defeated Arab armies, as was the case with Persia (modern Iran). This schism of the Caliphate (Sunni) denominations and the Shia extended to Indonesia and other non-Middle Eastern realms where Islam eventually prevailed. I find the message and methodology of Islam both repressive and dated with no contemporary relevance. Thus, to me, the only issue is what form of Christianity will I accept as meaningful in my life and why?

I have attended United Presbyterian churches in Pittsburgh; Pelham, New York; Princeton; and Fairfax and Williamsburg, Virginia. I am not an enthusiast of the rule of the elders and I have differences with a denomination with billions invested in the stock market. I feel my denomination could profit from some introspection and reform, but these differences are not sufficient to offset the benefits of corporate worship in the congregations I have joined. My personal faith is essentially nondenominational and follows the tradition of individual priesthood and scriptural interpretation. I am not a believer because I fear death. I am not sure whether everlasting life is an individually identifiable experience. I flatlined twice in January 2001, and the experience was not terribly revealing, uncomfortable, or frightening. If this life is all there is, I have had opportunities, I have helped others, and while I have enjoyed myself, I could have done better or could have done more, but I do not feel guilty about the life I have led. I have experienced moments of heaven on earth and some moments I do not wish to relive. I am not satisfied or finished, but I do not feel terrible frustration about what might have been.

I do wish I could feel more comfortable that this earth was on an upward slope, leading to a more fulfilling life of opportunity and value for my grandchildren. I am disturbed by a waning church that seems to be focused on an ancient God rather than a current God manifest in His new miracles. I am disturbed by "democratic" political systems that focus on the reelection of politicians, since raising funds for publicity is a full-time job, rather than allowing public servants to govern based on the interests of their constituents. And I am disturbed by a world of research that is controlled by academic or political structures that seem to look for researchers who have philosophical conformity. I do believe that if the clergy and scientists could develop mutually supportable consistency regarding proximate causes and ultimate causes, the politicians would mend their ways, even if they are pure pragmatists. We can do better, and I hope that, if required, our Creator will see fit to intervene again with a "sky-opening" event sufficient to reestablish His prominence in our earthly existence.

BIBLIOGRAPHY

Armstrong, Karen. *The Case for God.* New York: Alfred A. Knopf, 2009.

Bettenson, Henry, and Chris Maunder, eds. *Documents of the Christian Church.* Oxford: Oxford University Press, 1999.

Berlinski, David. *The Devil's Delusion.* New York: Basic Books, 2009.

Brown, Warren S., Nancey Murphy, and H. Newton Malony, eds. *Whatever Happened to the Soul?* Minneapolis: Augsburg Fortress, 1998.

Collins, Francis S. *Belief: Reading on the Reason for Faith.* New York: HarperCollins, 2010.

—. *The Language of God.* New York: Simon & Schuster, 2006.

Cramer, C. H. *Royal Bob: The Life of Robert G. Ingersoll.* New York: The Bobs-Merrill Co. Inc., 1952.

Davies, Paul. *The Mind of God.* New York: Simon & Schuster, 1992.

Dawkins, Richard. *The God Delusion.* London: Bantam Press, 2006.

—. *The Selfish Gene.* New York: Oxford University Press, 1976.

DeHamel, Christopher. *The Book: A History of the Bible.* London: Phaidon Press, 2001.

Diamond, Jared. *Guns, Germs and Steel.* New York: W. W. Norton & Company, 1999.

—. *Collapse: How Societies Choose to Fail or Succeed.* New York: Penguin Group, 2005.

Ehrman, Bart D. *Lost Scriptures.* New York: Oxford University Press, 2003.

—. *Misquoting Jesus.* San Francisco: Harper San Francisco, 2005.

Falk, Darrel R. *Coming to Peace with Science: Bridging the Worlds Between Faith and Biology.* Westmont, IL: Intervarsity Press, 2004.

Flew, Anthony. *There Is a God: How the World's Most Notorious Atheist Changed His Mind.* New York: HarperCollins, 2007.

Gingerich, Owen. *God's Universe.* Cambridge, MA: Belknap Press, 2006.

Goodspeed, Edgar, J. *Paul.* New York: W. W. Norton & Company, 1999.

—, trans. *The Apocrypha.* New York: Vintage Books, 1989.

Greene, Brian. *The Elegant Universe: Superstrings, Hidden Dimensions, and the Quest for the Ultimate.* New York: W. W. Norton & Company, 1999.

Harris, Sam. *The End of Faith.* New York: W. W. Norton & Company, 2004.

Hawking, Stephen, with Leonard Mlodinow. *A Briefer History of Time.* New York: Bantam Dell, 2005.

Hitchens, Christopher. *God Is Not Great: How Religion Poisons Everything.* New York: Hachette Book Group, Inc., 2007.

Johnson, Phillip E., and John Mark Reynolds. *Against All Gods: What's Right and Wrong about the New Atheism.* Westmont, IL: InterVarsity Press, 2010

Kaku, Michio. *Physics of the Future: How Science Will Shape Human Development and Our Daily Lives.* New York: Doubleday, 2011.

Kasser, Rudolphe, Marvin Meyer, and George Wurst, eds. *The Gospel of Judas*. Washington, DC: National Geographic Society, 2006.

Larson, Edward, and Larry Witham. "Scientists are still keeping the faith." *Nature* 386 (April 3, 1997), pp. 435–36.

Lennox, John C. *God's Undertaker: Has Science Buried God?* Oxford, UK: Wilkinson House, 2009.

Lincoln, Don. *The Quantum Frontier: The Large Hadron Collider*. Baltimore: Johns Hopkins University Press, 2009.

LeLoup, Jean-Yves. *The Gospel of Philip*. Rochester, VT: Inner Traditions, 2003.

Lewis, C. S. *The Complete C. S. Lewis: Signature Classics*. San Francisco: Harper San Francisco, 2002.

Mohler, R. Albert, Jr. *Atheism Remix*. Wheaton, IL: Crossway Books, 2008.

Polkinghorne, John. *Quantum Physics and Theology*. New Haven: Yale University Press, 2007.

Primack, Joel R., and Nancy Ellen Abrams. *The View from the Center of the Universe*. New York: Penguin Group, 2008.

Robinson, James M. *The Nag Hammadi Library*. New York: HarperCollins, 1990.

Sagan, Carl. *The Varieties of Scientific Experience*. New York: Penguin Press, 2006.

Sowell, Thomas. *A Conflict of Visions*. New York: Basic Books, 2007.

—. *Intellectuals and Society*. New York: Basic Books, 2009.

Sproul, R. C. *What Is Reformed Theology? Understanding the Basics*. Grand Rapids, MI: Baker Books, 2005.

Strobel, Lee. *The Case for a Creator*. Grand Rapids, MI: Zondervan, 2004.

Susskind, Leonard. *The Black Hole War*. New York: Little, Brown and Company, 2008.

Taleb, Nassim Nicholas. *The Black Swan.* New York: Random House, 2007.

—. *Fooled by Randomness: The Hidden Role of Chance in the Markets and Life,* 2nd ed. New York: Random House, 2005.

Tipler, Frank J. *The Physics of Christianity.* New York: Doubleday, 2007.

Ward, Keith. *The Big Questions in Science and Religion.* West Conshohocken, PA: Templeton Press, 2008.

www.ingramcontent.com/pod-product-compliance
Ingram Content Group UK Ltd.
Pitfield, Milton Keynes, MK11 3LW, UK
UKHW022223230426
12048UKWH00016BA/1035